SUS" FOR WRITING
MULTIPLE LANGUAGES

BBS and MSP

 www.trafford.com

North America & international
toll-free: 1 888 232 4444 (USA & Canada)
phone: 250 383 6864 ♦ fax: 812 355 4082 ♦ email: info@trafford.com

"SUS" FOR WRITING
MULTIPLE LANGUAGES

Dedicated to million kids, who tearfully

fight with their writing tools and wonder,

"Why writing couldn't be easier,

swifter and pleasing"

Preamble

'SUS' stands for **Sarma's Unified Script**. SUS, for all practical purposes, is an independent language with unique sound (or pronunciation and) distinctive script (or writing symbol). The people of various regions of this world have their own languages with distinctively different character. Knowingly or unknowingly they feel tremendous attraction for their language. In 1952 the people of East Pakistan did not accept and vehemently protested against the decision of their central government to change their mother language. They did not hesitate to sacrifice their lives for achieving their goal. In honour of their great sacrifice 21st February, the day they sacrificed their lives has been declared by the UN as International Mother Language Day.

Even though the above one is an example of extreme case, the people in general retain profound love and attraction for their mother tongue. Thus it is neither easy nor fair to ask the people to change their language. If one takes final and rigid decision on the basis of above reality, then there remains no necessity for conducting new studies, experiment or research on language such that the people can live with their existing languages for all time to come.

Same however, is not all true. People themselves change their languages. Quite often they accept new words from others languages and abandon theirs, if found unsuitable. At times they accept scripts of other language, in case the find their own scripts problematic. Change in words bring about some change in the language, or more truly, speaking language. Change of script, however, does not bring any change. The illiterate people cannot even feel this change.

In this age of science and technology new ideas are pouring in at every moment, research and experiments are being conducted in every sphere of life. As a consequence the world is being blessed with new invention and the people, with peace and prosperity.

Studies of various languages reveal that the languages were developed in the distant past in various areas in the situation prevailing in those regions and at time. Then those were modified, in which act, however, retaining the ancestors' achievements were given preference.

If someone with expertise in language is requested today to design and develop a language, definitely he would come out with one entirely different from the existing ones. It would differ from most or all of the existing languages, because it would be formulated on the basis of knowledge of science. Since science is a universal subject, there remains possibility that such a language would take care of not one but all the languages of the world. Such a language may be known as UNIFIED LANGUAGE.

In an endeavour to devise such a language the authors of this proposal could find out a language that is capable of bringing some positive change in the vocal aspect of any languages. What is more interesting is, it is capable of writing all languages of this world.

In the proposed Unified Language there are 40 letters including vowels and consonants. By using these one can speak most of the prominent languages of the world. Thus any language of the world can replace their alphabets by the alphabets of this language with, of course some positive change. This change however would bring about no or extremely little change in the pronunciation of some of their words. On the other hand it would totally eliminate the hazard we know as "spelling mistake".

The proposed Unified Language has got 40 writing symbols or scripts. These are stroke-based and extremely easy to memorize and write. The principle used in creating these scripts is so simple and logic-based that even if one forgets the scripts but can remember the basic principle, one can create those by himself. These scripts can be used in all languages, irrespective whether it is stroke based or line based, written from left to right or reverse, uses only letters or both letters and letter-signs etc. What is most encouraging is, the use of this script in any language brings about no, we repeat, absolutely no change in the speaking language.

The writing of the script is extremely easy, the letters are free from the criticism arising out of aesthetics (which happens due to human involvement) and it can be written at rapidly. Because of this quality the authors of this unified language found its scripts more potential and useful than its verbal component. Because of this reason the proposed Unified Language has been named as Unified 'Script', in place of Language.

In the past there were many endeavours to devise unified scripts, and there will be no dearth of such efforts in future. In order to differentiate those from this one, the term "Sarma" has been attached to it. Sarma is the family title of its proposers.

The best way to judge the inferiority or superiority of any new system is to present it before the users. The users are the best judge. After use they can make comparison and find out the relative advantages and disadvantages of those they use and the new one. In spite of such realities some people may feel reluctant to accept the new language or script on the plea that it might eliminate their traditionally-nurtured scripts. With profound honour for their decision these authors believe that in case found (i) swifter, easy and versatile, (ii) capable of saving the learner's unnecessary exhaustion and time and (iii) efficient in saving scarce resources of this world, this proposal would be given a scope to prove its worth.

CONTENTS

LIST OF FIGURES

Chapter I

INTRODUCTION

INTRODUCTION :

After birth what a child needs most is to express his needs. The child's mother is there to fulfil all her needs, many of which are complementary to the mother. Adults however, need some sort of media for exchanging ideas. After sign language, vocal language serves that purpose. It first appeared as a number of vocal sounds, later those were attached to feelings, known objects, animals and actions. In case of animals like cow, elephant, etc. they usually used to attach the sound created by these animals. In case of other entities like cloud, thunder etc., they imitated their sounds. Actions like attack, catching, digging, driving etc. also were earlier expressed through sounds. As of today we know those sounds as WORDS.

In order to express his ideas a man however, was in need of using many words. When a number of words was used one after another in a definite order that could create a sense. Such words expressing a single sense came to be known as sentence. And finally, the use of sentences led to the generation of LANGUAGE. Language is the fabric woven with sentences and letters act as the building blocks for words. Groups of people living in independent and discrete areas had to develop their own distinctive type of language for immediate use. The similarity, if there exist any, between the languages of two independent groups is rare and mere accidental. It happened so because various groups assigned sounds to feelings, objects, animals etc. according to their 'wish' and without any relation or logic.

Men are the inventors of their languages. In human society language appeared as blessing and profusely helped to establish closer relation between the members of the society. The same however, appeared as a barrier between the groups of people using different languages. The barrier exists still today. Something that can level this barrier is, Unified Language.

So long we discussed about the speaking or vocal language. This may be taken as one of the two major components of language. The other component is the writing symbol or Script. After men devised speaking language they could somehow run their day to day activities. The next thing they needed was how to document the vocal sound, such that those could cross the barrier of space and time. They were in need of carrying the language to a distant person and preserved for use in the coming days.

During this time the expert hunters used to teach the novice 'how to hunt animals'. To explain their techniques they drew sketches on the cave walls. That gave them the idea to document various sounds by drawing their 'pictures'. There was little problem in documenting the words they used for denoting animals or objects. However, drawing those indicating activities, emotions etc. was quite difficult. Naturally they had to draw the picture of such words arbitrarily and without any logical relation. It was easy for men to identify and remember the pictures representing animals and objects. But identifying and remembering the other types was quite tiresome. The situation turned still worse when the number of words started increasing day by day.

At this stage men discovered that the words in fact were composed of a number of "small single sounds". This 'single sound' or 'sound fragment' later came to be known as "Letter". They also discovered that in comparison with innumerable number of words the number of such letter was rather few.

The group of people living in isolated locations had absolutely no scope of forming a common understanding regarding the development of words or letters. So, various languages came up with their distinctly different type of writing symbols or scripts.

A complete set of these letters is known as Alphabet. For any language the scripts of the alphabet act as the basic building block. While some of the languages have devised simple scripts, some others have developed quite complex types. In some language the letters stand on a common ground or base line, in some language those hang from a line above, some writings start at left and proceed towards the right, some others follow the reverse direction and so on. Thus the barrier between the groups of people speaking in different language remained as it is even after the introduction of their scripts or writing components. Alike the speaking language, its written component also remained undecipherable to the outsiders.

In teaching language the first thing the children have to learn is the alphabet. In identifying the various sound components of letters the teachers picked up words containing those sounds. Also they picked up words representing animals, objects etc. because their pictures were relatively easy to recognize. What this trend caused in reality was, most, if not all of the letters sounded differently from the targeted basic sounds. That was the reason why various languages came up with alphabets having different sounding letters, even though they targeted for a common objective.

After men finalized letters the following task was to make visible symbols for each of them. At this time most of the users of languages became accustomed to using symbols for words. In finding out scripts they picked up few symbols from the vast number of symbols representing words and finished their job.

In the name of language, we, the descendants are continuing with what our ancestors created long ago with the names words, letters, alphabets and scripts. Some people who could not create their own scripts or discovered those 'problematic' accepted scripts of another language. During the age of colonization, some colonial masters compelled the people of their colonies to use their languages. Some of their colonies accepted the same and continue the same even after the end of colonization.

Some people find the language devised by their ancestors difficult to pronounce, slow and tedious to write and inconvenient in exchanging ideas. Still they love to stick to the gifted possession of their forefathers for emotional reason.

All these indicate that even if a "better media for exchange of ideas" or language is devised there is no guarantee that all people would accept it. This however, is no reason for those endeavouring to create new things to become discouraged. On the other hand, new ideas, thoughts and gadgets should always be welcomed. And if a new thing can prove its efficiency there is no reason why people would not accept it. Same is true for Unified language also.

'SUS' is the abbreviation for **Sarma's Unified Script**. As of today there exists no language that we can call Universal Language. The people living in various regions, for example in the forest, desert or mountain barriered lands, desolate islands etc. had to develop and use their own languages. That led to the birth of numerous languages. Even though men have learnt how to abolish and have really nullified these physical barriers, dissimilarities in their languages still act as barriers on way to exchange of ideas. This barrier exists not only in the field of vocal language, but also in written language.

In spite of the emotional attachment of some people for the creations of their ancestors, some other would continue their endeavours to find out or create new things with the objective of easing the problem of its users, to establish better and firmer relation between various communities and so on. Naturally, the same trend would also continue in the sphere of exchange of ideas through language.

In such an endeavour the first thing would be to find out the letters (i.e. basic sound fragments) with which man can generate the sounds they intend to do. There is no need to accept the ones which the common people find 'difficult' to pronounce. The number of such sounds should be as less as possible. Endeavours should be done to pick only the characteristically different sounds. Those making similar sounds should be avoided for the avoiding confusion misunderstanding.

After the sound fragments of the letters are finalized those may be classified on the basis of their creation mechanism inside human mouth. Their other characteristics, if any, should also be found out. Then those should be arranged in a definite order. Then the easiest and if possible, logical symbols would be chosen for each. This would give the Alphabet the Unified language.

SUS stands as abbreviation for **"Sarma's Unified Script"**. It started as an endeavour to devise Unified Language and it really did. Then it discovered two things : Number one, in spite of numerous problems the people in general have little intention to change their mother tongue(language) and Number Two : the written component or the scripts of SUS were found more efficient than the other component. In such a situation it was named Unified Script, and not Unified Language. It is inevitable that in future there will be numerous endeavours to find out more such unified languages and scripts. In order to differentiate those from this one 'Sarma', which is the family title of these authors have been added to it.

The alphabet of the proposed Unified Language has been created on the basic of 'distinguishable basic sound fragments'. The authors have picked up 40 different letters (including vowels and consonants) by using which it is possible to speak in most of the prominent languages. However, if necessity arises there is provision for incorporating new sounds for the purpose of speaking those languages.

In addition to 'letters' some languages use combined letters (consonants and vowels) and letter-signs (mostly vowel signs) as modifiers to the principal letters. In the proposed SUS, there are provisions for using such modifiers also. In some languages some letters at times are pronounced for a longer time. The same word (i.e. word spelt by the same letters) gives different meaning when pronounced differently. The scope for such pronunciation has also been provided in SUS.

After finalizing the sounds of the letters, SUS has designed stroke based symbol or script for each of them. At present the number of script is 40. However, by using the principle applied here this number can be increased to 80 and beyond. It may be mentioned that 80 is a much higher number than the number of letters used by most of the languages, excepting however, Chinese and Japanese alphabets. In Chinese and Japanese languages words are considered as letters and vice versa.

The principle used in creating the proposed scripts is extremely simple. Some basic guidelines were formulated as the basis of designing the scripts. These are :

(i) The number of strokes will be as less as possible,

(ii) The strokes will be of straight lines only,

(iii) In general the strokes would start at the bottom and move upward, or start at the left and move towards the right,

(iv) The lines would join together at right angles only,

(v) If there is any change of location of any stroke, then it would take place in the clockwise direction only etc.

The application of these principles has rendered the SUS script so easy that once a learner can understand the basic principles and their applications, he can later create those by himself, even if he forgets the scripts. The scripts are simple and have wide scope of manipulation to satisfy the needs of all types of languages. Thus SUS can be used for writing :

(i) Stroke based language,

(ii) Line based language,

(iii) Language written from left to right,

(iv) Language written from right to left,

(v) Language having only one type of letters,

(vi) Language having both capital and small letters,

(vii) Language using vowel sings as modifiers,

(viii) Language having both long and short pronunciations etc.

One of the great advantage of SUS is, if the scripts of any language are replaced by SUS, there happens absolutely no change in its vocal component or pronunciation. By hearing the read out version of a language written in SUS script, the user of a language would not even be able to understand if was read from the original scripts of the language or from its SUS version.

A mere look at the SUS scripts may convince the common reader that these are extremely easy to write, free from 'change in aesthetics' due to human involvement and that, these can be written much more speedily. With such qualities the scripts of the proposed Unified language would prove to be much more useful than its verbal component. For this reason the proposed unified language has been named as Unified 'Script', in place of Language.

Chapter II

BRIEF HISTORY OF LANGUAGE

INTRODUCTION :

Men communicate with one another through language. Language has got two major components : Speaking and Writing. Sign language may be considered as its third component which is used by the people with hearing disability. There is absolutely no relation between the linguistic sign of a language and its meaning. Thus the meaning of various linguistic signs or word is correctly understood exclusively by its users and those bear no meaning for the users of other languages. In various languages completely different words may be used to mean the same object or animal. Thus a dog is known as 'dog' in English, 'perro' in Spanish, 'sobaka' in Russian, 'inu' in Japanese, 'kukur' in Bengali, 'sarameya' in Sanskrit etc.

The scientific study of language is known as linguistics. It has a number of branches like : (i) Phonetics, (ii) Phonology, (iii) Morphology, (iv) Syntax, (v) Semantics, (vi) Pragmatics etc.

Phonetics : It It is related with the physical properties of sounds. It has three subfields. (a) Articulatory, (b) Acoustic phonetics and (c) Auditory phonetics.

(a) Articulatory phonetics : It explores how the human vocal apparatus produces sounds.

(b) Acoustic phonetics : It studies the sound waves produced by the human vocal apparatus.

(c) Auditory phonetics : It examines how speech sounds are perceived by the human ears.

Sounds of language are the fragment of sound having special character. It is pronounced within a fraction of a second, even though it can then be prolonged with a different sound. The fraction of sound having individualistic character is known as letter. The complete set of letters used in any language is known as alphabet. Sounds which change their character are known as consonant sound or letter. On the other hand, those which do not change character even if prolonged are known as vowel sound or letter.

None of the letters like d, o, and g has any meaning. However, when the tree letters are combined together to create common sound, it means one type of domestic animal. The combined sound 'dog' is known as a word. Also various words may join together to give an entirely different meaning.

Sounds are produced due to vibration of the vocal cord. Most of the sounds are produced during the expulsion of air from the lungs. Then the same is modified in the vocal tract between the larynx and the lips. It is also possible to pronounce sounds while taking in air. Various sounds are modified due to the manipulation of the throat by the larynx, lips, tongue etc. Sounds can also be produced by means other than expelling air. At times air is trapped in the space between the front of the tongue, the back of the tongue and the palate and then released. Such sounds are known as clicks

Phonology : Phonology is concerned with how various sounds function in a particular language. Even though every letter is supposed to have a definite pronunciation, in some sound the pronunciation depends upon its location in the word. For example, in English language, k is usually pronounced as c, when it is used at the beginning of a word (example, cut) and it is pronounced with aspiration (i.e. with a puff of breath). But when this sound occurs at the end of a word (viz. tuck) there will be no aspiration. Phonetically speaking, the aspirated k and un-aspirated k have different sounds, but the English speakers do not even feel it. It happens so because English language does not make any phonological distinction between the aspirated and un-aspirated k. On the other hand, in Hindi language the sound difference due to aspirated and un-aspirated letters is considered phonetic and phonological distinction. In Hindi 'kal' (with un-aspirated k) means 'time' and 'khal' (with aspirated k, pronounced like 'kh') means 'skin'.

Morphology : It deals with the structure of words. The linguists consider the morpheme as the basic units of grammatical structure. So they consider the word cats to have composed with two morphemes, cat and s. And the meaning of the two comes to be : (01) Cat – 'feline animal', and (02) (Cat)-s, 'more than one'.

In the same way the word Antimicrobial has three morphemes, 'Anti' meaning 'capable of destroying microorganisms', 'microbe', meaning microorganism, and -ial, a suffix that makes the word an adjective. The study of these smallest grammatical units and the various ways in which they combine into words is called known as morphology.

Syntax : It deals with the structure of phrases and sentences. Syntax is the study of how words combine to make sentences. The order of words in sentences varies from language to language. In English language, syntax follows a general order of "subject-verb-object". Example : "The cat (subject) ate (verb) the rat (object)." If the words are placed differently like, The rat cat ate the, ate the at the rat etc. these bear no meaning. However, the above mentioned order is used differently in different languages. Also more than one order is followed in some languages, where each of the order gives different meaning.

Also in many cases the words are not directly combined into sentences, but rather into intermediate units, called phrases. These phrases are then combined into sentences. In the sentence "The man found his lost son" contains at least three phrases: "The man", "found" and "his lost son". The hierarchical structure that groups various words into phrases and phrases into sentences, serves important role in establishing relations within the sentence.

Semantics: It deals with the study of meaning. While the fields of language study mentioned above deal primarily with the form of, Semantics is the field of study of the meaning of various linguistic elements. Semantics primarily deals with the meaning of individual morphemes. It also studies the meaning of the constructions that link morphemes to form phrases and sentences.

Pragmatics : It studies the interaction between language and the contexts in which it is used.

DIALECT : A dialect means a variety of a language spoken by an identifiable group or subgroup of people. Traditionally, linguists have applied the term dialect to geographically distinct language varieties. However, in current usage the term includes speech varieties characteristic of other socially definable groups. Determining whether two speech varieties are dialects of the same language, or whether they have changed enough to be considered as distinct languages, has often proved a difficult and controversial decision. At times the linguists cite "mutual intelligibility" as the major criterion in making their decision. If two speech varieties are not mutually intelligible, then the speech varieties belong to different languages. And if they are mutually intelligible but differ systematically from one another, then they are considered as dialects of the same language. All the linguists do not follow this definition. Since many levels of mutual intelligibility are in existence, the linguists need to decide at what level speech varieties should be considered mutually intelligible. In practice however, it is quite difficult to establish.

Dialects primarily develop because of limited communication between different parts of a community that share one language. In the above circumstances, changes that take place in the language of one part of the community do not spread in other areas. If contacts remain confined in discrete areas for a long period, sufficient changes will accumulate to make the speech varieties mutually unintelligible. When this occurs and especially if it is accompanied by the socio-political separation of a group of speakers from the larger community, it usually leads to the recognition of separate languages. The different changes that took place in spoken Latin in various regions of the Roman Empire, for example, eventually led to the development of distinct modern Romance languages, like, French, Spanish, Portuguese, Italian and Romanian.

PIDGIN LANGUAGE : A pidgin language is the language used for communication by groups that have different native tongues. It develops when people speaking different languages are brought together and forced to develop a common means of communication without allowing sufficient time and scope to learn each other's languages properly. Usually the pidgin language derives most of its vocabulary from one of the languages. Its grammatical structure, however, will either be highly variable, or reflect the grammatical structures of the speaker's native language. The plantation societies in the Caribbean and the South Pacific have originated many pidgin languages. Tok Pisin is the major pidgin language of aborigines of Papua New Guinea.

CLASSIFICATION OF LANGUAGE :

Estimates of the number of languages spoken in the world today vary depending on where the dividing line between language and dialect is drawn. For instance, linguists disagree over whether Chinese should be considered a single language because of its speakers' shared cultural and literary tradition, or whether it should be considered several different languages because of the mutual unintelligibility of, for example, the Mandarin spoken in Beijing and the Cantonese spoken in Hong Kong (*see* Chinese Language). If mutual intelligibility is the basic criterion, current estimates indicate that there are about 6,000 languages spoken in the world today. However, many languages with a smaller number of speakers are in danger of being replaced by languages with large numbers of speakers. In fact, some scholars believe that perhaps 90 percent of the languages spoken in the 1990s will be extinct or doomed to extinction by the end of the 21st century. The 10 most widely spoken languages, with approximate numbers of native speakers, are as follows: Chinese, 1.2 billion; Arabic, 422 million; Hindi, 366 million; English, 341 million; Spanish, 322 to 358 million; Bengali, 207 million; Portuguese, 176 million; Russian, 167 million; Japanese, 125 million; German, 100 million. If second-language speakers are included in these figures, English is the second most widely spoken language, with 508 million speakers. *See also* Indian Languages.

Linguists classify languages by following two major systems : (01) Typological and (02) Genetic.

(01) TYPOLOGICAL : In the typological classification system various languages are organized according to the similarities and differences in their structures. The languages which share the same structure belong to the same type. For example, even though there remain significant differences between the two languages Mandarin Chinese and English, these two belong to the same type, when considered in terms of structure of sentence. Both languages follow the same structure or basic word order, which is 'subject-verb-object'.

(02) GENETIC : In genetic classification languages are grouped into families on the basis of their historical development. The languages which descend historically from the same common ancestor form a Language family.

ROMANCE LANGUAGES FAMILY : The languages included in this family are : French, Spanish, Portuguese, Italian and Romanian. All these languages have descended from the Latin language. Latin, in turn, belongs to a larger language family, Indo-European. The origin of Indo-European lies in Proto-Indo-European.

INDO-EUROPEAN LANGUAGES FAMILY : In Europe the most widely spoken languages are Indo-European languages. These are also spoken in western and southern Asia. In Europe there are many varieties of languages like : (i) Germanic languages (viz. English, German and Dutch) and (ii) Scandinavian languages (viz. Danish, Norwegian and Swedish). At one time the Celtic languages (viz. Welsh and Gaelic) were spoken over a large part of Europe. But now these are in use only in the western fringes. The Romance languages descending from Latin are the lone survivor of a somewhat more extensive family, Italic.

Many languages were spoken in the Baltic countries. At present however, only two survive and these are: Lithuanian and Latvian. The languages generally spoken in eastern and central Europe are the Slavic languages. Important Slavic languages are : Russian, Ukrainian, Polish, Czech, Serbo-Croatian etc.

Two branches of Indo-European languages, viz. the Greek and the Albanian languages are still spoken in the Balkan Peninsula. In the Caucasus the Armenian language constitutes another single-language branch of Indo-European language.

Another surviving language of the Indo-European family is Indo-Iranian Language. It has two sub branches, (i) Iranian and (ii) Indo-Aryan (Indic).

> (i) IRANIAN : Iranian languages are spoken mainly in south-western Asia. Various versions of this language are known by the names, Persian, Pashto (spoken in Afghanistan) and Kurdish.

> (ii) INDO-ARYAN : Indo-Aryan languages are spoken in the northern part of South Asia i.e. Pakistan, northern India, Nepal, Bangladesh and Sri Lanka. Various branches of this language are : Hindi-Urdu, Bengali, Nepali and Sinhalese.

DRAVIDIAN FAMILY LANGUAGE : In South Asia, in addition to the Indo-Aryan branch of Indo-European, there exist two other language families. The Dravidian family language is dominant in southern India with names, Tamil and Telugu. The Munda languages represent the Austro-Asiatic language family in India and contain many languages, each with relatively small numbers of speakers.

SINO-TIBETAN LANGUAGE FAMILY : The Sino-Tibetan language family are found in China, much of the Himalayas and parts of Southeast Asia. The major languages of this family are : Chinese, Tibetan, and Burmese.

SOUTHEAST ASIA LANGUAGE FAMILY : One important language family of Southeast Asia is the Tai language. Tai and Thai languages are spoken in Thailand, Laos and southern China. The Miao-Yao or Hmong-Mien language are spoken in isolated areas of southern China and northern Southeast Asia. The languages spoken in Malay Peninsula, islands to the southeast of Asia, Madagascar, Pacific islands, Easter Island etc. belong to Austronesian languages family, formerly known as Malayo-Polynesian. The various languages of Austronesian languages family are : Malay. This language is known as "Bahasa Malaysia" in Malaysia and "Bahasa Indonesia" in Indonesia. It is also known as Javanese, Hawaiian and Maori. Maori is the language of the aboriginal people of New Zealand. Some people of the coastal areas and offshore islands of New Guinea speak Austronesian languages. However, most people of the main island speak in a number of languages collectively referred to as Papuan language.

AFRICAN LANGUAGE FAMILIES : The languages of Africa belong to four families: (i) Afro-Asiatic, (ii) Nilo-Saharan, (iii) Niger-Congo and (iv) Khoisan. However, the linguists are not still sure about the genetic unity of Nilo-Saharan and Khoisan.

(i) AFRO-ASIATIC : Afro-Asiatic languages occupy most of North Africa and part of south-western Asia. The family consists of several branches. The Semitic branch includes Arabic, Hebrew and some languages of Ethiopia and Eritrea. The Chadic branch, spoken mainly in northern Nigeria and adjacent areas, includes Hausa. It is one of the two most widely spoken languages of sub-Saharan Africa. Other subfamilies of Afro-Asiatic family are Berber, Cushitic and the now-extinct language of the ancient Egyptians.

(ii) NILO-SAHARAN : The best-known Nilo-Saharan language is Masai, spoken by the Masai people in Kenya and Tanzania. The Nilo-Saharan languages are also spoken in eastern Africa, in regions between the area covered by the Afro-Asiatic and the Niger-Congo languages.

(iii) NIGER-CONGO : The Niger-Congo family languages covers most of sub-Saharan Africa. The family includes languages like Yoruba, Fulfulde, Bantu, Swahili and Zulu. Swahili is spoken by wide population in eastern Africa. The Nilo-Saharan languages are spoken mainly in the eastern Africa, in an area in between those covered by the Afro-Asiatic and the Niger-Congo languages.

(iv) KHOISAN : The Khoisan family languages with name Nama language (formerly called Hottentot) are spoken in the south-western corner of Africa.

LANGUAGE FAMILIES OF THE AMERICAS :

The languages of the Americas have been divided into a large number of families and isolates. According to one linguist, all the American languages can be grouped into just three super families, even though most others differ. The prominent language families are (i) Inuit-Aleut (Eskimaleut), (ii) Na-Dené languages, (iii) Algonquian and Iroquoian, (iv) Siouan, (v) Uto-Aztecan, (vi) South America etc.

(i) Inuit-Aleut (Eskimaleut) : This family language stretches from the eastern edge of Siberia to the Aleutian Islands and across Alaska and northern Canada to Greenland, where one variety of the Inuit language, Greenlandic, is an official language.

(ii) Na-Dené languages : The main branch of Na-Dené languages comprises the Athapaskan languages. It occupies much of north-western North America. The Athapaskan languages also include a group of languages in the south-western United

States, one of which is Navajo.

(iii) Algonquian and Iroquoian families : Languages of the Algonquian and Iroquoian families are the major indigenous languages of north-eastern North America.

(iv) Siouan family : The Siouan language family is one of the main families of central North America.

(v) Uto-Aztecan : The Uto-Aztecan language family extends from the south-western United States to Central America. It includes Nahuatl, the language of the Aztec civilization and its modern descendants. The Mayan languages are spoken mainly in southern Mexico and Guatemala.

(vi) South America : Major language families of South America are Carib and Arawak in the north and Macro-Gê and Tupian in the east. One of the national languages of Paraguay is Guaraní. It is an important member of the Tupian family. In the Andes Mountains the dominant indigenous languages are Quechua and Aymara.

Chapter III

LETTER WITH SINGLE SOUND

Language started with vocal sounds. Man shouted to express his needs, his emotions and directives for others. Men sorted the meaningless sounds to denote particular object, animal or action and familiarized the same to all members of the community. That initiated their local language.

Man can create sound because of vocal cord and his ability to make it vibrate. The sound created due to vibration passes through the throat and escapes through the mouth or nose. On its way it may be interfered by various organs in a number ways. We shall discuss hereunder the essential sound making and manipulating organs and their operations.

In order to explain what we want to, we need to mention simultaneously various organs and their various operations. In order to make it simple we have used some legends as shown in Fig. No. 3.01 :

Fig. No. 3.01 SOUND CREATING ORGANS, OPERATIONS AND LEGENDS :

ORGANS	OPERATION	LEGEND
Throat	Closing or obstructing	C
	Opening	O

Tongue	Funnelling of shaping inverted crescent	F
	Vibrating	V
	Taking in air	I
	Expelling out air	E

ORGANS AND THEIR OPERATIONS :

(a) Volume of mouth-cavity and shape of the LIPS (abbreviated as C-L): After being generated at the vocal chord the sound passes through the throat and mouth. This sound can be changed by changing the internal volume and shape of the mouth cavity. This is done mostly by the changing the size and shape of the open lips.

(b) THROAT (abbreviated as Tr) : The throat can change a sound by closing (Tr-C) and opening (Tr-O). By closing it can create pressure of air and then create sound by sudden release.

(c) TONGUE (abbreviated as Tn): The tongue can change sound in several ways like creating obstruction or closing (Tn-C) and channelling air by imitating Funnel (Tn-F). Obstructions are done by placing the tip of the tongue on the upper plate of the mouth. The sound is also changed due to the form of the tip of the tongue, which may be (i) flat forward, (Tn-F) (ii) flat reverse (Tn-R), (iii) hard pressed and then released (Tn-H), (iv) lose pressed and then released (Tn-L) etc. Also the sound can be changed due to the placing of the tongue at different locations of the upper part of the mouth. The hind part of the upper mouth may be identified as hind part, the middle as middle part, front as front part and the near the teeth as Teeth-root. These four positions will be abbreviated as : Hind part - 1, Middle part - 2, Front part -3 and Teeth root – 4.

(d) NOSE (abbreviated as Ns): While talking men at times use the nasal route for releasing part of air (Ns-O). The sound changes its nature if the nasal route is <u>closed</u> (Ns-C).

(e) Movement of AIR (abbreviated as Ar-I) : Sound may be produced both at the time of taking in air (Ar-I) and expelling out (Ar-E). Generally a "HA" like sound is added during expelling air.

After knowing the various organs and operations we shall go for investigating the various sounds man can generate. The following table shows such conditions of creation. We have shown pronunciation of these sounds through English alphabet. It may be mentioned that English alphabets cannot take care of all such sounds. In such cases we have mentioned part of known words, where the sound is pronounced exactly or nearly like that. It should also be mentioned that theoretically speaking it is possible to pronounce all the sounds shown in the table. In practice, however, men use only a few of those and avoid all those which are difficult to pronounce or do not have perceivable difference. Thus, even though there are (9 X 15 =) 141 probable sounds, men roughly use about 40, i.e. only 28%.

Various probable sounds to be created by various operations and manipulations of human organs and the sounds actually created have been shown in **Fig. No. 3.02**.

Fig. No. 3.02 SONUD POSSIBILITIES AND FREQUENTLY USED SOUNDS WITH MANIPULATORS :

SOURCE	STRESS LEVEL -1		STRESS LEVEL -2		
Position	Air taken in (Ar – I)	Air Expelled (Ar-E)	Air taken in (Ar-I)	Air Expelled (Ar-E)	

			Nasal Route Open	Nasal Route Closed	Nasal Route Open	Nasal Route Closed	Nasal Route Open	Nasal Route Closed	Nasal Route Open	Nasal Route Closed	Nasal R
			Ns-O	Ns-C	Ns-O	Ns-C	Ns-O	Ns-C	Ns-O	Ns-C	
LIPS	01	A	ANG	HA	MN	HRA	----	----	----		- - - -
	02	a	----	----	----	----	----	----	----		-
	03	AA	----	----	----	----	----	----	----		-
	04	EE	----	----	----	HRI	----	----	----		-
	05	U	----	----	----	----	----	----	----		- - - -
	06	E	----	----	----	----	----	----	----		- - - -

| | 07 | O | ---- | OY | ---- | ---- | ---- | ---- | ---- | - - - - |

| THROAT | KA | ---- | KHA | ---- | GA | ---- | GHA | ---- | - - - - |

TONGUE (Touched)	01	TA	----	THA	----	DA	----	DHA	----	N A
	02	LA	----	----	----	----	----	----	----	- - - -
	03	ta	----	tha	----	da	----	dha	----	- - - -

TONGUE	01	CHA	----	CHA	----	JA	----	JHA	----	----
(H. pressed)	02	SA	----	SHA	----	-----	----	----	----	----

TONGUE									
RA	----	RHA	----	----	----	----	----	-	
(Loose pressed)								-	

LIPS	PA	----	FA	----	BA	----	BHA	----	MA

In the above Figure, the sounds shown against LIPS are those sounds which are created by the vocal cord and then, manipulated by the mouth cavity due to the action of the lips. These are known as Vowel- sounds. The first sound A (pronounced like 'oug' in Fought) is a neutral sound that normally exists with all the consonant sounds. If this sound is pronounced while expelling air, it is pronounced as "HA".

Even though there 7 X 9 = 63 possibilities of sounds in this group, most of the languages use only 13, i.e. about 20.6%. It is possible for sounds beyond these possibilities to exist, but those might be extremely difficult to pronounce.

The sounds generated by Throat, Tongue and Lips shown above are known as Consonant sounds. Even though there are as many as 8 X 9 = 72 possibilities of such sounds, the number of the most commonly used sounds is 27, i.e. 37.5% only. Other sounds are not generally used for the reasons mentioned above. Thus by every likelihood a language can run smoothly with a total number of 13 + 27 = 40 letters. For the sake of ease of learning and memorizing by the children, the number of letters / scripts should be kept as less as possible. The Alphabet of SUS has been designed with these 40 letters.

SOUND OF THE LETTER :

The most important quality of a letter is, it must be pronounced independently. The SUS letters have got this quality. It would have been the best if all other languages could have letters with this quality. Unfortunately it did not happen so in case of most of the languages. The reason is simple. The experts did not get the scope of designing the letters. On the other hand, it was done by their ancestors who lacked this knowledge. And in most cases the common people could not think of ignoring the creation of their ancestors, whatever inadequate or inefficient those could have been.

It is extremely difficult to convey the sound of Letters through written language. Its scope is naturally limited by the range available in any language. For instance, there are 26 letters in English alphabet. Some of the English letters have more than one sound or pronunciation. Thus C may be pronounced as Ch (like Ch in Chalk) or Ka (like Co in Cotton). On the other hand all the 40 letters of SUS have got 40 independent and distinctly different sounds or pronunciations. So, it is evident that it would not be possible to express all these sounds by a language having 26 letters.

In **Fig. No. 3.03** below we have mentioned examples from English language in order to express the sounds of the 40 SUS letters. In some cases, however, we could not find the exact match and have mentioned similar ones only.

Fig. No. 3.03 PRONUNCIATION (SOUND) OF SUS ALPHABET :

SL.	LETTERS OF UNIFIED SCRIPT SHOWN IN ENGLISH ALPHABETS	EXAMPLES FOR NEAREST PRONUNCIATION (Pronounced like)
01	O	'ough' in Fought, 'o' in Cot, 'o' in Knot.
02	ONG	'ong' in Wrong, 'ong' in Strong.
03	HA	'Ho' in Honolulu, 'Haw' in Hawker, 'Ho' in Holly.
04	MN	It does not have any sign in English language, but its nearest substitute is, expressing by placing a 'n' after the letter. This is the pronunciation of the consonants with the nasal orifice closed.
05	RHA	'ra' in Broiler, 'ro' in Trolley, 'rau' in Fraud.
06	A	'a' in Bat, 'a' in Cat, 'a' in Fat, 'a' in Mat.
07	U	'U' in Umpire, 'u' in But, 'u' in Cut.
08	I	'I' in Iran, 'ee' in Bee, 'i' in Beautiful.
09	HRI	'ri' in British, 'hri' in Christian.

10	U	'u' in Put, 'oo' in Root, 'ou' in Route.
11	E	'e' in Pet, 'e' in Kettle, 'a' in Mate.
12	O	'oa' in Boat, 'oa' in Coat, 'oa' in Goat.

13	KA	'Ka' in Karachi, 'Co' in Coronation, 'Cau' in Caution.
14	KHA	'Kho' in Khorashan.
15	GA	'g' in Agfa, 'g' in Agra, 'Go' in Gorilla.
16	GHA	'Gh' in Ghost,

17	TA	't' in Utmost, 't' in Eight,
18	THA	(Near to and not exactly)
19	DA	'Do' in Doll, 'D' in Door, 'tt' in throttle.

20	**DHA**	'Dh' in Dhaka,
21	**NA**	'No' in Nottingham,
22	**LA**	'Lo' in Lottery, 'Lo' in Lord,
23	**ta**	'th' in Teeth.
24	**tha**	'th' in Author.
25	**da**	(Near to and not exactly) 'Th' in Thou,
26	**dha**	……… …… (Not found)
27	**CHA**	(Near to and not exactly) 'Ch' in Chair.
28	**CHHA**	…………………(Not found)
29	**JA**	'Jo' in Jolly, 'Geo' in Georgia, 'ze' for harmonize.
30	**JHA**	(Near to and not exactly) 'Jha' in Jhansi.
31	**SA**	'ss' in Dismiss.
32	**SHA**	'ssio' in Admission.
33	**RA**	'Ro' in Rotten.

34	**RHA**	'ro' in Protein.

35	**PA**	'Po' in Polish.
36	**FA**	'gh' in Rough
37	**BA**	'b' in February.
38	**BHA**	've' in Love.
39	**MA**	'Mau' in Mauritius, 'Mo' in Moral.
40	**OY**	'oy' in Boy.

LETTERS WITH MULTIPLE SOUNDS :

In some languages one letter has got more than one sound or pronunciation. Such provision of multiple pronunciation lead to 'spelling mistake". In **Fig. No. 3.04** we have shown the sounds of SUS letters in English alphabet. Also we have shown a number of the same or similar sounding letters from Bengali and Arabic.

Fig. No. 3.04 SUS LETTERS (Sounds expressed through English letters) AND SIMILAR

SOUNDING LETTERS FROM BENGALI AND ARABIC LANGUAGE :

SUS	1. KA	2. KHA	3. GA	4. GHA	5. RA
BENGALI	ক	থ	গ	ঘ	র
ARABIC	ق	خ	غ, ك	---	ر
SUS	6. CHA	(07) CHHA	(08) JA	(09) JHA	(10) LA
BENGALI	চ	ছ	জ	ঝ	ল
ARABIC	----	ث, ص	ج , ذ, ظ	ن	ل
SUS	(11) TA	(12) THA	(13) DA	(14) DHA	(15) NA
BENGALI	ট	ঠ	ড	ঢ	ন
ARABIC	ط	----	----	----	ن
SUS	(16) PA	(17) FA	(18) BA	(19) BHA	(20) MA
BENGALI	প	ফ	ব	ভ	ম
ARABIC	----	ف	ب	----	م
SUS	(21) Ta*	(22) Tha*	(23) Da*	(24) Dha*	(25) RHA
BENGALI	ত	থ	দ	ধ	ড়
ARABIC	ت	----	د, ض	----	----
SUS	(26) SA	(27) SHA	(28) HRI	(29) ANG	(30) HRA
BENGALI		শ	ষ	০ং	র ফলা

ARABIC	س	ش	-----	-----	------
SUS	(31) EE	(32) U	(33) A	(34) O	(35) OY
BENGALI	ই	ঊ	অ	ও	য়
ARABIC	ى	----	----	ء	----
SUS	(36) AA	(37) E	(38) a	(39) HA	(40) MN**
BENGALI	আ	এ	য ফলা আা	হ	------
ARABIC	ا	ع	▬▬▬	ه ,ح	▬▬▬

Left over (not required in SUS) Bengali letters : ঙ, ঞ, ণ, য, ষ, ঐ, ঊ, ঐ, ঔ

Left over Arabic letters : Nil

ADVANTAGE AND DISADVANTAGE OF SUS (SOUNDS) LETTERS :

We have mentioned that SUS letters can be accepted by any language. Accepting SUS alphabet means, replacing the existing alphabet of that language by the 40-lettered SUS alphabets. There are both advantage and disadvantage of accepting the SUS alphabet.

DISADVANTAGE :

(i) If accepted the learners would need to learn some additional letters beyond the number of their own alphabet. Thus the users of English language may have to learn (40 − 26 =) 14 new letters. In Bengali there are (Consonant 35 + Vowel 10 + Vowel-sign 13 =) 58 letters and signs. In this case the learners would not have to learn (58 − 40 =) 18 letters. In Arabic there are (consonant and vowel 28 + Vowel sign 8 =) 36 letters. So, the learners would have to learn (40 − 36 =) 4 new letters.

ADVANTAGE :

(i) Those users who would need to learn some additional letters (sounds) would be able to pronounce these additional sounds.

(ii) In the languages mentioned above (i.e. English, Bengali and Arabic) there are more than one letter with the near-same or similar sounds. This creates confusion leading to a problem known as "spelling mistake". In SUS, each of the letters has distinctly different and only one sound. So, there is no possibility of "spelling mistake" in SUS language.

Chapter IV

SCRIPTS FOR LETTERS

At the dawn of civilization some people started drawing the picture of various words as its substitute. The same could not continue for long because they discovered that the huge number of words could neither be expressed by pictures nor easy to memorize. As a solution they initiated the idea of isolating and writing the basic fragments of words or syllables. By this way they got letters and the symbols used to denote the letters were known as scripts.

Sounds of the letters constitute only half of any language. In order to attain permanency and be communicable the language needs the written symbols of the letters, known as scripts. After discussing the sounds of the letters of the SUS alphabets we shall discuss about its Scripts.

The above information might prove why we do not find any logical relation between the sounds and scripts of the letters. While some of the languages are written by strokes, many others are written by long lines. Some incorporate shapes like circles, half circles, triangles, squares, dots etc. Some languages are written with letters standing on a base line (for example, English, Arabic etc.), in some languages the letters hang from above or run between two parallel lines (for example, Bengali). When machines like type writer, computer, printing machine etc. are used for typing letters, the letters are seen clear and undistorted. But when those are written by hand, due to human involvement circles turn to ellipses, ellipses to double lines, triangles into bent lines and so on. In the long handwriting the letters used in forming a word are connected with one another and those in general change their original forms. This create great problem in deciphering. Needless to mention that, any mistaken or wrong meaning may result in disaster.

With the above realities in mind the SUS scripts have been designed with utmost care and to satisfy wide range of requirements. We have mentioned that the way in which men started to write scripts there was absolutely no scope of maintaining logical relation between the sound and the symbol (script). At present it is possible to design various scripts presenting the way the human organs need to work to generate it. Even though interesting from the scientific point of view, such scripts would neither be easy to write nor would have any importance for the common people lacking in the knowledge of sound generation.

In the above situation the authors of SUS followed a different principle. It included the following :

(i) The number of strokes will be as less as possible,

(ii) The strokes would be of straight lines only,

(iii) In case of prolongation the strokes would start at the bottom and move upward, or start at the left and move towards the right,

(iv) The lines would join together at right angles only,

(v) Whenever there will be any change of location it would take place in the clockwise direction only.

And finally, the logical relation between the sounds and the changing forms of the scripts will be maintained on the basis of the location of the letters in the table of the alphabet.

Before we go for designing the scripts we would like to see the complexities existing in the letters of some languages. For reference we shall take into consideration scripts from English, Bengali and Arabic languages.

COMPARING VARIOUS SCRIPTS : In order to have a better understanding of the complexities in writing letters we present hereunder some letters having the same or similar pronunciation from 3 languages in **Fig. no. 4.01**.

Fig. No. 4.01 COMPLEXITIES OF WRITING VARIOUS SCRIPTS :

LANGUAGE	SCRIPT	SCRIPT	SCRIPT	SCRIPT	SCRIPT	SCRIP
ENGLISH	Ka	Kha	Ga	Gha	Ta	Th
BENGALI	ক	খ	গ	ঘ	ট	ঠ
ARABIC	ق	خ	غ	ك	ط ت	-----
ENGLISH	Da	Dha	Na	Cha	Chha	Ja
BENGALI	ড	ঢ	ন	চ	ছ	জ
ARABIC	ض	----	ن	----	ث	ظ ,ح ,ذ
ENGLISH	Jh	Ra	Rha	La	Ta	Pa
BENGALI	ঝ	র	ড়	ল	ট	প
ARABIC	ز	ر	----	ل	----	----
ENGLISH	Fa	Ba	Bha	Ma	Ong	Ha
BENGALI	ফ	ব	ভ	ম	ৎ	হ
ARABIC	ف	ب	----	م	----	

LETTER AND SCRIPT :

Even though the success of any language profusely depend upon an efficient script, the history of the development of scripts reveal why no language could ever get that. In spite of numerous problems the experts of various languages did not have the courage to reform the same because of the emotional attachment of the common people with the gift of their ancestors.

In reality however, the vocal language (related with the sound component of the letters) is entirely different from the written language, which is related with writing component of the letters. Sound component is the life of any language. If there happens any change in the sound component, the language is changed, or in other words it suffers from death. Same is not the case with its writing component. The writing component is the mere media for documentation and communication. It does not have any relation with the subject matter or the emotion it carries. For example : a song sung by a singer may be recorded in cassette recorder, digital recorder or a mobile phone. The person enjoying the output (i.e. vocal song) may not even understand the difference between the carrying medias, so long there is no change in the quality of sound.

In the past sounds were recorded in the old-styled phonograph and the listeners were amazed to hear the 'excellent' sound. By today's experience obtained due to digital recorders we know, how 'inferior' those sounds were. And today we cannot imagine what excellent type of sound we might get in future with the invention of new gadgets.

What has been said in connection with recording and reproduction of sound is exactly similar to the design of scripts. Today the user of a language might be aware about the problems in their scripts, but one does not bother much because one finds no alternative option. Some of the notable problems various scripts may have are the following :

(i) The script may be of such nature that those cannot be written swiftly.

(ii) The writing may turn clumsy and non-decipherable, when written rapidly.

(iii) The letters may not occupy equal space.

(iv) It may be difficult to memorize and recreate the scripts.

Now we shall explain the above points in brief.

(01) THE SCRIPT MAY BE OF SUCH NATURE THAT THOSE CANNOT BE WRITTEN SWIFTLY : It is generally thought that a line based script is slower than a stroke based one. Quite often it is thought that a line-based script will be swifter because the line runs in one direction only. And a stroke-based one will be slower because the writer needs to shift the pen with every new stroke.

In practice, however, in the line scripts one has to make shapes, curves, angles etc. and the writer needs to shift back the pen every time he needs to create these. Also he needs to use modifiers (various vowel signs, dots, punctuations etc.) and need to pick up the pen for this purpose. A stroke-based script however, is free from all these hazards. True that the writer needs to shift the pen every time he uses a new stroke. That however, keeps his letters free from distortion or confusion. In such a situation the speed of a stroke based script depends largely upon the number of strokes in each word. SUS has been designed as a stroke-based script with minimum number of strokes. And in most cases the number of strokes is only FOUR, even though many of the letters are written by THREE strokes.

(02) THE WRITING MAY TURN CLUMSY AND NON-DECIPHERABLE, WHEN WRITTEN RAPIDLY : In this age when men are increasingly depending on machine printing, one of the principal role of hand writing is to transfer message which will be read out or deciphered later. Here the question of speed is equally important as correct reading. Disasters may take place if the handwritten messages are not deciphered correctly. English handwriting has a line-based script and hence it is supposed o be written quickly. The problem is, as soon as the writer increases the speed the writings turn too clumsy to read out. It may be mentioned that most of the hand written messages are read by person other than the writer. In order to take care of this situation many users of English at present use the Capital Printing version for writing. This script is definitely slow because it is mostly stroke-based, but it is also dependable because of less possibility of distortion because of being 'stroke-based'. SUS has preferred the most dependable option.

(03) THE LETTERS MAY NOT OCCUPY EQUAL SPACE : A study of three languages viz. English, Bengali and Arabic might reveal that in none of these languages the letters occupy equal space. Thus in English 'I' occupies minimum space and 'W' or 'M', the maximum. Even though all letters of the printing version of capital English letters stay between the top and bottom margins, many of the words in its other 3 versions (i.e. Printing small, Writing capital and small) either crosses the lower margin, or leave vacant space above. In case of Bengali,

the letters in general hang from the upper margin and extend below the lower margin, specially when the he modifiers (vowel-signs) are used. All these create considerable problems for the learners and in machine printing. The case with Arabic letter also is similar. In comparison with those, all the SUS scripts occupy equal space and none ever crosses the margins.

(04) IT MAY BE DIFFICULT TO MEMORIZE AND RECREATE: If one remembers the history expressing how the sound and writing components of various languages came into being, one can understand why some of the scripts are so peculiar to look at. The peculiarity may be noticed more clearly by the users of other languages. After long time use the users of any language become accustomed and then love to see even the most peculiar letter of their language. The difference or comparative superiority of any script can be known only after comparison with unbiased mind.

THE CHANGED ROLES OF HANDWRITING :

The role of handwriting changes with time. Some important aspects of this change are the following :

(i) There was a time when handwriting was considered as one of the appreciable achievement of men. Many competitions were held and prizes, given for good hand writing. Today what men care for is, clear and quick handwriting, and not the beautiful ones.

(ii) There was a time when handwriting was the only mode of documentation of information. Thus it was essential for all writings to be clear, readable and free from confusion. In spite of the invention of many sound recording gadgets, this requirement is equally valid till this day. What has changed, is the time available or allotted for such writing. What is needed now is a quick system of writing that might not lead to any confusion.

(iii) In the past teaching handwriting and language was considered in many societies as a respectful job. Those living on this profession enjoyed profuse honour and financial advantage in the society. Proficiency in speaking and writing language was considered as a hard job. In fact, in some societies the experts endeavoured to make the language quite complex to read and write and thus keep it out of the reach of the common people. In India teaching Sanskrit language was at times considered as the sacred profession of

33

the higher caste people. They rendered this language, specially its grammar so complex and difficult that the learners got frustrated. As a consequence they abandoned that language and opted for a local language named "Prakrita". Later Bengali was developed in combination of the two.

Even though endeavours were made to make Bengali simple, the same could not come out successful because of the conservative outlook of the experts, specially those belonging to the old generations. Bengali letters came from Sanskrit. Sanskrit language should be admired for one reason. In that old age they devised letters whose sounds, in most cases, resemble the basic minimum fraction of sound. What was extremely problematic was its grammar and use of similar sounding words. Also the scripts were quite difficult to write. Bengali language reformed the grammar and made it easy. They also modified the scripts. But in place of being easier those turned even more complex. And the worst thing is, Bengali inherited the burden of "multiple letters with similar sounding" from Sanskrit.

Countries like Japan, China, Korea etc. use stroke based scripts. In this type they use huge number of letters, most of which act also as letters. When the number of letters increase the learners find hard days. Still the local learners have to learn those because they are left with no alternative. If a student is given an option to choose between a language with several thousand letters and another with 30/50 letters, there remains possibility that he would choose the second one.

In comparison between the Long handwriting and Stroke type writing, the writing of the first one has got some advantages. But since this type incorporates various shapes like triangle, circle, ellipse, straight lines slanting at various angles, curved lines with various curvatures etc., these are subject to change due to human touch. Also there remains wide possibility for being clumsy, illegible, confusion-prone and undecipherable by others. However, there is wider scope of adding artistry to this type of script. On the other hand, there is less scope of adding artistry to the stroke-based scripts.

Chapter V

SCOPE OF "SUS" AS A LANGUAGE

In this age, when the civilization is constantly exerting pressure on men for increasing use of keyboards and recording gadgets for transferring messages, writing has turned to the secondary media of transmission. However, any misinformation due to confusion or any other reason in the handwriting may prove extremely disastrous. In such a situation, the efficiency of a language depends upon (i) how clearly it can be spoken by using minimum number of sound-fragments or letters, (ii) how easily and speedily it can be written, (iii) how the handwritten messages can be made free from ambiguity and confusion and (iv) how the reading and writing of languages can be made a pleasing act for the children. The grandfathers' preference for "pearl-like hand writing" does not have any appeal in the modern society, nor does the same serve any practical purpose. Modern gadgets in fact have nearly eliminated the need for calligrapher or designers of handwriting.

In such a context, SUS has been designed as a language with minimum number of letters, each fulfilling the character of "individualistic fragment of sound". After ensuring this for the reading purpose, SUS has designed the simplest and easiest type of script for them, such that (i) the learners can learn those within days, (ii) those can be written easily and swiftly and (iii) the output becomes free from ambiguities and confusions. After doing this the authors were amazed to discover one additional quality of the scripts, it was found that these scripts can be used in writing almost all types of languages, including those using principal letters, vowel-signs, other signs etc. Also it was found suitable for writing those writing from left to right or in the reverse direction.

Most of the prominent languages use any one of the following two modes of writing :

(01) Writing only with letters (i.e. Vowels and Consonants) and

(02) Writing with letters (i.e. Vowels and Consonants) and Vowel signs.

English is the example of the first mode. Reading and writing this type of language is extremely easy. The words are formed by placing the letters side by side. Even though it does not serve any great purpose, the English follows a system of using Capital letters at the beginning of a new line and in certain words. For this reason, however, the learners need to learn another 26 letters and the type machines, 26 keys.

Example of a language using the second mode is Bengali. In addition to using normal vowels this language also use vowel-signs before, after, above, below or both before and after the consonants. Such uses create considerable problem for the typing and printing machines. The extension of any letter beyond the margins also creates problem.

After finalizing the scripts the authors discovered that, while these scripts can be used in writing the letters of the unified language, the same scripts could be used to write both English and Bengali. As additional advantage, the scripts keep all the vowel signs confined within the margins even in case of Bengali.

The tribe known as "Hausa" and living in Northern Nigeria used to speak in a language known as Hausa. Since they used to live in a small and confined area they did not feel much necessity of the writing script. After the British occupied Nigeria the people belonging to this tribe dispersed all over and could feel the need for the written script. By this time the British introduced English as their state language. Immediately the Hausa people accepted English alphabet to write Hausa since it was convenient and readily available.

During 1947-1971, Pakistan was facing problems in retaining good relations between its two wings, East Pakistan and West Pakistan. The two wings were separated by a distance of about 1000 miles. The people of two wings were fighting for the declaration of their respective language as the state language. The languages for which the people of the two wings fought were, Urdu and Bengali. As a solution, a proposal was made for forming a common language (Lingua-franka) by using Urdu alphabet. The people of the then East Pakistan did not accept it because of the following reasons : (i) It in fact proved biasness for one language, Urdu. (ii) After a language accepts the alphabet of a third language, many of the words, construction of sentence, grammar etc. of that language gets entry in the host language. It happened so in case of Hausa language also.

It indicates that if any language changes its scripts and accepts that of another language, then its users may suffer from the following type problems : (i) inferiority complex because of the thought that they had to accept other's script, (ii) possibility that words and grammar of that language might encroach theirs and (iii) the pronunciation of some words might change.

It is a fact that, while using a language the users of various languages in fact enjoy the gifts of their ancestors. With the same however, they also suffer from the pains if there lies any serious problem in any language. In the contemporary world, when the user of one language get the scope to see many other languages at times wonder saying, "Why did they make the scripts of our language so complex ?", "What made them to make the pronunciation so difficult ?", "Why did they keep so many letters to pronounce the same sound only to throw us amidst hazards of spelling mistake ?" etc.

Even though science has enlightened every sphere of human life, it could not do much in eliminating the constraints present in various languages. Now if the users of a language decide to follow "alphabets constituting of the basic sound-fragments" in place of the different type of alphabets created by their ancestors, then they would have to accept something similar to what the authors have mentioned above as "Unified Language". In accepting this language, there is absolutely no reason for the people of any country or region to suffer from inferiority complex because as of today "Unified language" does not really exist. In this language the letters are composed of the bare minimum and basic sound fragments only. These are not the property of the people belonging to any group, region or race. On the other hand all human being reserve the right to use it, because it is what science is destined to invent. Also in this case there is no fear of the flow of alien words or grammar from the guest language. As of today the Unified Language does not have any word or grammar of its own.

The Unified Language has been formed with minimum number of letters and the number is 40. In course of accepting it, if the experts of any language discover that all the sounds of their language have not been included in its alphabet, then there is provision for increasing it. This number can easily be increased to 80 and beyond.

Studies reveal that even though various languages have given various names to its letters, while using in words they use its basic sound fragment only. Thus letter P in English alphabet is pronounced as PEE, but the sound it adds to the word is "PA", which is the bare minimum and basic individualistic fragment of sound.

Now the question is, is there any possibility that a language accepting Unified Language would lose some of its previous character ? The answer is "Yes". The Unified language has been designed such that there can arise no confusion and unnecessary complications. However, such complications already exist in some languages. For example, the use of similar sounding letters in English or Bengali has created the "spelling mistake" hazards. So, if the alphabets (sound) of these languages are replaced by those of the Unified language then the inevitable change in character that would take place is the "elimination of spelling mistake hazard". Similarly the Unified language would be able to remove other confusions and complications also.

Thus, in English language, words like (01) Cot, (02) Caught, (03) Kot and (04) Kought pronounce the same thing. In English only two of the above 4 are correct and those give different meaning. If English accepts Unified language then the word pronounced as 'Kot' would have one and only spelling. Similarly in Bengali there are two words : (01) 'Apan' (আপন),using dantya Na and meaning own and (02) 'Apan' (আপণ) using Murdhgya Na and meaning shop. The difference in pronunciation of these two words is so insignificant that many would not even be able to perceive the difference while hearing. The teacher however, is there to find out the spelling mistake. If Bengali accepts the Unified language there would remain no scope of this mistake.

Even though the acceptance of Unified language would remove all confusions and unnecessary complications from any language, there is possibility that it might bring changes in the pronunciations of some words. It is possible that such changes would not be acceptable to the experts. The nicest thing in the Unified language is, it can easily take care of this situation,

A language can accept only the scripts (i.e. written letters and not their sounds) of the Unified Language to write their language. If this is done then the vocal form of the language would remain exactly the same as before with all its previous limitations, confusions and advantages. While writing however, they would soon discover that they can write their language swiftly and their remains no scope of confusion or ambiguity in deciphering those. Also the teacher finds no reason to complain about 'bad handwriting'. There remains immense possibility that the children would discover writing as a pleasurable job.

Chapter VI

LETTER FOR "SUS"

Like the letters of any other language, the SUS letters also have got two major components : (01) The sound (or pronunciation) and (02) Script (or writing symbol). SUS alphabet is constituted of 40 letters including Vowels and consonants. These have been shown in **Fig. No. 6.01** below :

Fig. No. 6.01 SOUNDS (PRONUNCIATION) OF "SUS" LETTERS :

Group	.0	.1	.2	.3	.4
01	KA	KHA	GA	GHA	RA
02	CHA	CHHA	JA	JHA	LA
03	TA	THA	DA	DHA	NA
04	PA	FA	BA	BHA	MA
05	Ta*	Tha*	Da*	Dha*	RHA
06	SA	SHA	HRI	ONG	HRA
07	EE	U	A	O	OY
08	AA	E	a	HA	MN**

* Sounds marked with asterisks cannot be properly pronounced by English letters.

** It indicates uttering of any sound with closed nasal orifice, similar to use of 'n' used after any English consonant.

In the above Table, Letters from KA to SHA are consonants and the remaining are Vowels. However, there is no need to irritate the beginners by telling them which one is vowel and which one, consonant. Any learner can learn the language with full satisfaction without knowing the differences between the two. Language like English use only letters and no vowel-sign and it seemingly creates no constraint.

DESIGNING SCRIPTS FOR THE SOUNDS :

The SUS scripts or letters have been designed with extreme care such that those could be easily remembered and recreated. As a deviation from the conventional letters which use curve lines, various shapes, lines at various angles etc., all the lines used in "SUS" are straight lines, those run either horizontally or vertically and join only at right angles. In order to write all the letters of "SUS" what one would need are :

i.   1 Horizontal line (used always in the central location),

ii.   1 vertical line (used in 4 different locations),,

iii.   1 free short vertical line (used in 4 locations) and

iv. 1 short horizontal line (used in 2 locations, above and below).

These are shown in **Fig. No. 6.02** below.

Fig. No. 6.02 ALL ONE NEEDS FOR WRITING "SUS" ALPHABETS :

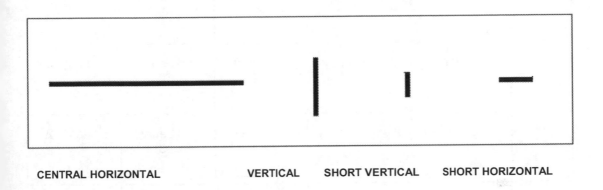

CENTRAL HORIZONTAL   VERTICAL   SHORT VERTICAL   SHORT HORIZONTAL

MEMORIZING THE SCRIPTS :

The learners first need to memorize the sounds or pronunciation of "SUS" Letters. The parents or teachers may tell them the pronunciations directly or through sound recorder. Colored books with pictures of known objects, animals or activities containing the specific sound-fragment would be helpful. By this time the learners should also learn digits and counting. They would need to memorize the letters with the help of logic provided in terms of numbers. All the letters would be presented in groups of five, where the first letter would act as the group-head.

REMEMBERING LOCATION OF LETTER :

After the learners have memorized the sounds of the letters, they would have to know the relative positions of the letters in terms of numbers, as shown in **Fig. No. 6.03**. Thus they would find that 'JA' is 2.2, 'HRI' is 6.2, 'MA' is 4.4 etc.

Fig. No. 6.03 REMEMBERING "SUS" SCRIPTS BY LOCATION :

Group	.0	.1	.2	.3	.4
01	1st Letter **1.0**	2nd Letter **1.1**	3rd Letter **1.2**	4th Letter **1.3**	5th Letter **1.4**
02	1st Letter **2.0**	2nd Letter **2.1**	3rd Letter **2.2**	4th Letter **2.3**	5th Letter **2.4**
03	1st Letter **3.0**	2nd Letter **3.1**	3rd Letter **3.2**	4th Letter **3.3**	5th Letter **3.4**
04	1st Letter **4.0**	2nd Letter **4.1**	3rd Letter **4.2**	4th Letter **4.3**	5th Letter **4.4**
05	1st Letter **5.0**	2nd Letter **5.1**	3rd Letter **5.2**	4th Letter **5.3**	5th Letter **5.4**
06	1st Letter **6.0**	2nd Letter **6.1**	3rd Letter **6.2**	4th Letter **6.3**	5th Letter **6.4**
07	1st Letter **7.0**	2nd Letter **6.1**	3rd Letter **7.2**	4th Letter **7.3**	5th Letter **7.4**
08	1st Letter **8.0**	2nd Letter **7.1**	3rd Letter **8.2**	4th Letter **8.3**	5th Letter **8.4**

STARTING TO WRITE :

After they memorize all the letters and understand their relative positions from the above Table, they can go for writing. All the "SUS" scripts are contained within a square box. The First Letter of each of the group act as the group head. As per relative position the group heads have been marked like **1.0, 2.0, 3.0, 4.0, 5.0** etc. **.0** indicates that it would exist independently and would not take the help of any other element. All the letters representing a group have been designed with one central horizontal line and one of more pieces of vertical lines and 1 free vertical line. The 4 locations where the vertical lines would meet the central line has been shown in **Fig. No. 6.04.**

Fig. No. 6.04 LOCATIONS OF VERTICAL LINE CHANGING IN CLOCK-WISE DIRECTION :

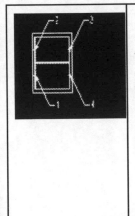

The group heads are written by using one horizontal line at the middle and then by attaching 1, 2, 3 or 4 nos. half-sized vertical lines at the two extreme ends. The principle followed is, the first line will be joint at location 1, second at location 2 and so on. The Lines would start from down to up and then from left to right. The operation shown by 1, 2, 3 and 4 would continue in a clockwise manner, as shown in the figure.

MAKING THE GROUP LEADERS :

It is possible to make a number of letters (group-head) by attaching the half-vertical lines to the central horizontal line at 4 different locations. The "SUS" alphabet is made of 40 letters. It is possible to make 40 letters by using (40 / 5 =) 8 group heads. It has already been mentioned that "SUS" is capable of writing most, if not all, prominent languages. Some languages may have bigger number of letters in their alphabets. In Fig. 6.05 we have shown as many 16 group-heads. These may create letters numbering up to (16 X 5 =) 80. There remains further scope for increasing the number. However, most of the prominent languages have alphabets with less than 80 letters. The 16 group heads have been shown in **Fig. No. 6.05.**

Fig. No. 6.05 SYMBOLS OF THE FIRST LETTERS OF 16 GROUPS :

Group 1 - Letter 1	Group 2 - Letter 1	Group 3 - Letter 1	Group 4 - Letter 1
Group 5 - Letter 1	Group 6 - Letter 1	Group 7 - Letter 1	Group 8 - Letter 1
Group 9 - Letter 1	Group 10 - Letter 1	Group 11 - Letter 1	Group 12 - Letter 1
Group 13 - Letter 1	Group 14 - Letter 1	Group 15 - Letter 1	Group 16 - Letter 1

Fig. No. 6.06   4 LOCATINS FOR FREE VERTICAL LINE :

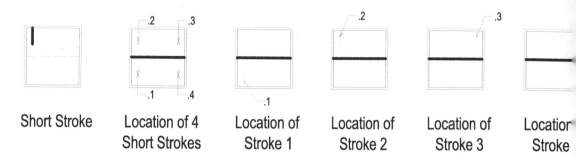

| Short Stroke | Location of 4 Short Strokes | Location of Stroke 1 | Location of Stroke 2 | Location of Stroke 3 | Location Stroke |

The five letters of each group would be formed in the following manner :

(01) First letter :   The letter acting as 'group head' and designated as 1.0, 2.0, 3.0, 4.0 etc. will be made with zero (no) stroke.

(02) Second letter : This letter designated as 1.1, 2.1, 3.1, 4.1 etc. will have the stroke at location 1.

(03) Third letter :   This letter designated as 1.2, 2.2, 3.2, 4.2 etc. will have the stroke at location 2.

(04) Fourth letter : This letter designated as 1.3, 2.3, 3.3, 4.3 etc. will have the stroke at location 3.

(05) Fifth letter :   This letter designated as 1.4, 2.4, 3.4, 4.4 etc. will have the stroke at location 4.

LETTERS FOR "SUS" LANGUAGE :

The 40 lettered alphabet of SUS language along with group number, approximate pronunciations in English letters etc. have been shown in Fig. No. 6.06.

DESIGNING LETTERS FROM THE GROUP HEADS :

The first letter of each group has been marked as 1.0, 2.0, 3.0 etc., indicating that these need zero, or no other element as assistant. Now, four letters with similar sounds will be designed from each of the group heads. For this purpose the small free vertical line would be placed at four different locations, marked as 1, 2, 3 and 4 as shown in **Fig. No. 6.07** below. As mentioned earlier, in this case also the locations would change in clock-wise direction.

Fig. No. 6.07 SOUNDS (PRONUNCIATION) OF "SUS" ALPHABET :

Gro up		.0	.1	.2	.3	.4
01	Script (Writing symbol)					
	Sound or Pronunciation given in English alphabet	(ka)	(kha)	(ga)	(gha)	(ra)
02	Script					
	Sound	**(cha)**	**(chha)**	**(ja)**	**(jha)**	**(la)**
03	Script					
	Sound	**(ta)**	**(tha)**	**(da)**	**(dha)**	**(na)**
04	Script					
	Sound	**(pa)**	**(fa)**	**(ba)**	**(bha)**	**(ma)**

05	Script					
	Sound	**(ta*)** Pronounced like ট of Bengali	**(tha*)** Pronounced like থ of Bengali	**(da*)** Pronounced like দ of Bengali	**(dha*)** Pronounced like ধ of Bengali	**(rha*)**
06	Script					
	Sound	**(sa)**	**(sha)**	**(hri)**	**(ang)**	**(hra)**

07	Script					
	Sound	**(ee)**	**(u, oo)**	**(a)**	**(o)**	**(mn)**
08	Script					
	Sound	**(aa)**	**(e)**	**(a)**	**(ha)**	**(oy)**

The five letters of each group would be formed in the following manner :

(01) First letter : The letter acting as 'group head' and designated as 1.0, 2.0, 3.0, 4.0 etc. will be made with zero (no) stroke.

(02) Second letter : This letter designated as 1.1, 2.1, 3.1, 4.1 etc. will have the stroke at location 1.

(03) Third letter : This letter designated as 1.2, 2.2, 3.2, 4.2 etc. will have the stroke at location 2.

(04) Fourth letter : This letter designated as 1.3, 2.3, 3.3, 4.3 etc. will have the stroke at location 3.

(05) Fifth letter : This letter designated as 1.4, 2.4, 3.4, 4.4 etc. will have the stroke at location 4.

WRITING NUMBERS (DIGITS) BY "SUS" :

"SUS" has been designed with the objective of assigning the basic single fraction of sound to the letters. It is applicable to any language even without changing the pronunciation of their letters. Similar is the case with the Digits or Numbers. In this case the sounds (pronunciation) of digits used in various languages shall be retained as it is. SUS would only suggest for changing the script (writing symbol) with a much simpler one. SUS has devised 10 new scripts for 10 digits.

For this purpose "SUS" would use 4 simple strokes only as shown below :

(i) 1 vertical line,

(ii) 1 small horizontal line to be used in 2 locations and

(iii) 1 free horizontal line to be used in 2 locations.

ALL ONE NEEDS FOR WRITING "SUS" DIGITS :

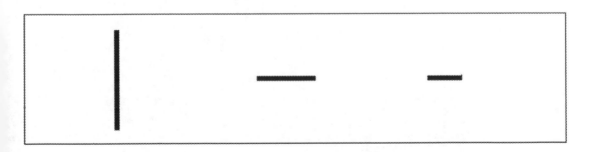

VERTICAL LINE   SMALL HORIZONTAL LINE   FREE HORIZONTAL LINE

The various locations in which the Small and Free horizontal lines would be used have been shown in **Fig. No. 6.09.** Also the SUS scripts for all the 10 digits have been shown in **Fig. No. 6.10.**

Fig. No. 6.09 USE AND LOCATIONS OF STROKES FOR WRITING NUMBERS :

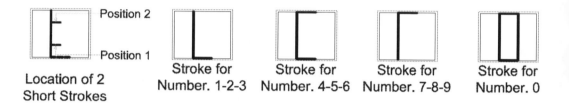

Location of 2
Short Strokes

Stroke for
Number. 1-2-3

Stroke for
Number. 4-5-6

Stroke for
Number. 7-8-9

Stroke for
Number. 0

Fig. No. 6.10   SCRIPTS FOR 10 "SUS" DIGITS :

1	2	3	4	5	6	7	8	9	0

Chapter VII

USING "SUS" IN ENGLISH LANGUAGE

INTRODUCTION :

In broad comparison with the English alphabet the "SUS" scripts have got the following specialities :

(i) In this alphabet there is minimum number of letters and the number is 40,

(ii) One type of sound is expressed by only one letter and

(iii) Only the letters can create words, without taking the help of any modifier (e.g. vowel signs).

On the other hand, English alphabet is composed of 26 letters (having independent sound) and the language does not need the help of any modifier. In such a situation if SUS alphabets are introduced in English then the learners might notice the following :

(i) An increase of (40 – 26 =) 14 letters. This would enable them to pronounce 14 more sounds.

(ii) Some of the English letters have more than one sound that gives birth to "wrong spelling". On the other hand in SUS alphabet one letter has got one and only one sound. So, if English alphabet is replaced by that of SUS, there would remain no scope for 'wrong spelling'.

(iii) In spite of some advantages, definitely there will be some disadvantage because the learners would discover the spelling of some of their known words differently and the grammar also would chnage.

In such a situation let us abandon the idea of introducing SUS alphabet in English. But we can easily think of replacing the English letters by the SUS scripts. We have already mentioned that this replacement would not bring absolutely no change in pronunciation, formation of sentence, grammar etc. of the English language.

INTRODUCING SUS SCRIPT :

Let us suppose that the learners of English language has already memorized the 26 letters. Now the first job they would have to do is to divide the 26 letters in groups of 5 and assign a number for each of the letter on the basis of its position in the table. The Table has been shown in **Fig. No. 7.01**.

Fig. No. 7.01 ASSIGNING LOCATIONS FOR ENGLISH ALPHABET :

		.0	.1	.2	.3	.4
1	LETTER	A	b	c	d	e
	LOCATION	$1._0$	$1._1$	$1._2$	$1._3$	$1._4$
2	LETTER	F	g	h	i	j
	LOCATION	$2._0$	$2._1$	$2._2$	$2._3$	$2._4$
3	LETTER	K	l	m	n	o
	LOCATION	$3._0$	$3._1$	$3._2$	$3._3$	$3._4$
4	LETTER	P	q	r	s	t
	LOCATION	$4._0$	$4._1$	$4._2$	$4._3$	$4._4$
5	LETTER	U	v	w	x	y
	LOCATION	$5._0$	$5._1$	$5._2$	$5._3$	$5._4$

6	LETTER	Z				
	LOCATION	$6._0$				

The identity of various letters on the basis of their positions shown in the above Table are : **a = 1.0, q = 4.1, x = 5.3 etc.**

WRITING ENGLISH LETTERS :

The next job now is to write the scripts for each letter. Since the number of letters is only 26, we shall need only 6 group heads, which we shall select from the table of group heads shown earlier. Those who might find it difficult to memorize the various group heads may remember the principle followed in creating those. After knowing the group heads it is possible to create 4 more letters under each group by placing the short "Free stroke" in 4 different locations, which start at left below and rotates in clock-wise direction. he next thing the learner would have to learn is to substitute the English letters by the SUS scripts. The sounds (pronunciation) of 26 English letters (no change) along with the scripts representing them have been shown in **Fig. No. 7.02** below.

Fig. No. 7.02 ENGLISH LETTERS WRITTEN IN SUS SCRIPT :

	.0	.1	.2	.3	.4
	a	b	C	d	e
1					
	$1._0$	$1._1$	$1._2$	$1._3$	$1._4$

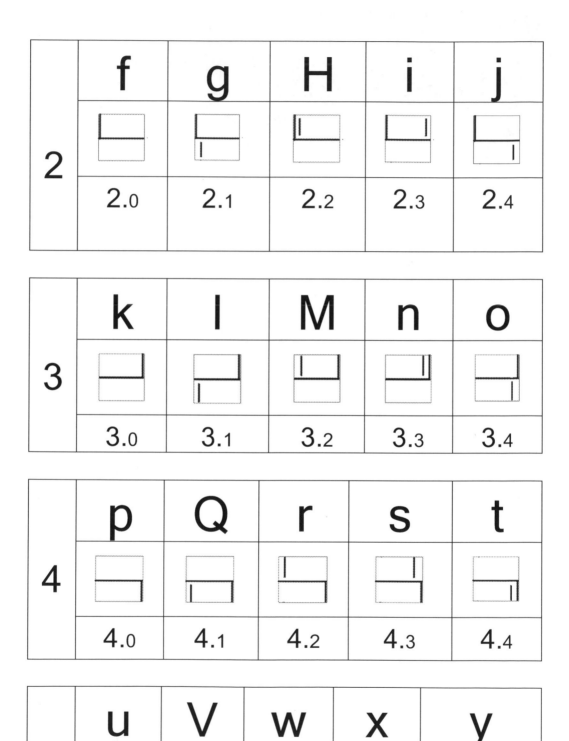

2	f	g	H	i	j
	2.0	2.1	2.2	2.3	2.4

3	k	l	M	n	o
	3.0	3.1	3.2	3.3	3.4

4	p	Q	r	s	t
	4.0	4.1	4.2	4.3	4.4

u	V	w	x	y

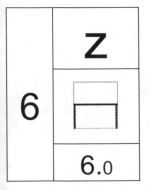

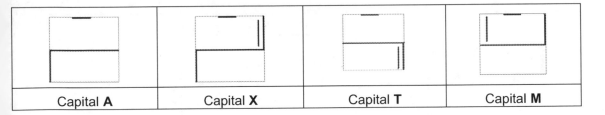

CAPITAL LETTERS :

For writing English capital letters a small horizontal has to be used above as shown in **Fig. No. 7.03.**

Fig. No. 7.03 CAPITAL LETTERS :

Capital **A**	Capital **X**	Capital **T**	Capital **M**

SCRIPTS FOR PRINTING :

What we have discussed above are the scripts for writing. This is generally done with fixed-width tools like Pen or Pencill. When the machine printers and publishers use these in books, they beautify those by providing Fonts of various types and nature. However, there is absolutely no problem in making nice-looking and artistic versions of SUS scripts.

SAMPLE SENTENCES :

It is no wonder that to any user of English language the SUS alphabets shown in this book would seem like strangers and those of English, as known relatives. This is quite natural because, by all means SUS is a new comer and hence, a stranger. Using it for a few weeks, however, would turn these also as close relatives. However, while comparing the close relative (English script) with the stranger (SUS script) with unbiased mind, one might notice the relative simplicity of this script to remember and write. Once the logic and principle in which the various SUS letters have been designed is understood, one does not need much effort to remember or recreate those.

Fig. No. 07.04. EXAMPLES :

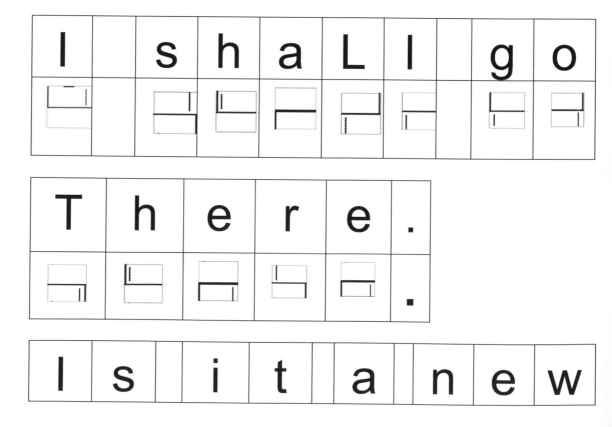

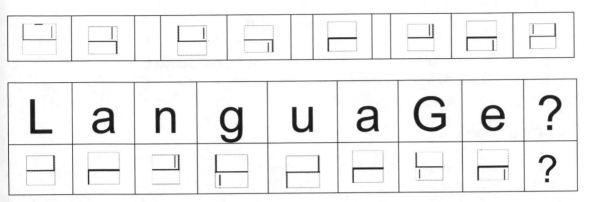

CONCLUSION :

We have shown above how efficiently the SUS script can be used in writing English language, keeping the oral part of the language, pronunciation, grammar etc, as it is. By following the same principle it is also possible to write all the languages (like, Italian, Spanish, German, French, Hausa etc.) that use English alphabet by using the SUS script.

Chapter VIII

USING "SUS" IN BENGALI LANGUAGE

INTRODUCTION :

In Bengali language there are 45 Principal letters comprising of 35 consonants and 10 Vowels. In addition there are 13 modifiers. Also there are combined letters. Even though this language is a bit complex in comparison with English, it is possible to fulfil all the requirements of this language through SUS. We shall present the solutions in the following ways : (01) Writing the Principal letters and (02) Writing Modifiers.

(01) WRITING 45 PRINCIPAL LETTERS :

Following the principle followed in case of English, the 45 principal letters of Bengali will be divided into 9 groups each with 5 letters and the Group head for each will be designated. Then the identity of each letter according to its position in the table would be found out. This has been shown in **Fig. No. 8.01.**

Fig. No. 8.01. IDENTITY FOR THE PRINCIPAL LETTERS :

Group	.0	.1	.2	.3	.4
01	ক (Ka) 1.0	থ (Kha) 1.1	গ (Ga) 1.2	ঘ (Gha) 1.3	ঙ (Uma) 1.4
02	চ (Cha) 2.0	ছ (Chha) 2.1	জ (Ja) 2.2	ঝ (Jha) 2.3	ঞ (Nia) 2.4
03	ট (Ta) 3.0	ঠ (Tha) 3.1	ড (Da) 3.2	ঢ (Dha) 3.3	ণ (Na) 3.4

04	ত	থ	দ	ধ	ন
	(ta∗)	(tha∗)	(da∗)	(dha∗) **4.3**	(na∗)
	4.0	4.1	4.2		4.4

05	প	ফ	ব	ভ	ম
	(Pa)	(Fa)	(Ba)	(Va)	(Ma)
	5.0	5.1	5.2	5.3	5.4

06	য	র	ল	শ	ষ
	(ja)	(ra)	(la)	(sha)	(SHa) **6.4**
	6.0	6.1	6.2	6.3	

07	স	ড়	ঢ়	য়	হ
	(Sa)	(Rha)	(Rhha)	(Ya)	(Ha)
	7.0	7.1	7.2	7.3	7.4

08	অ	আ	ই	ঈ	ও
	(a)	(AA)	(EE)	(EEE)	(O)
	8.0	8.1	8.2	8.3	8.4

09	উ	ঊ	এ	ঐ	ঔ
	(OO)	(OOO)	(E)	(OI)	(OU)
	9.0	9.1	9.2	9.3	9.4

In the above Table various Letters have got identities like, 'Ka' (☐) is 1.0, 'La' (ল) is 4.0 and so on. After learning the identities of the Bengali letters, the learner would have to replace those by SUS scripts. This has been shown in **Fig. No. 8.02**

Fig. No. 8.02 BENGALI MODIFIERS (VOWEL-SIGNS AND OTHERS):

MODIFIERS	আ	ই	ঈ	উ	ঊ
Pronunciation in English	AA	EE	EEEE	U	UU
SUS script used as modifier					

MODIFIERS	এ	ঐ	ও	ঔ	হসন্ত
Pronunciation in English	E	OI	O	OU	Hasanta
SUS script used as modifier					

MODIFIERS	ঋফলা	য ফলা	র ফলা
Pronunciation in English	HRI fala	AA	RA fala
SUS script used as modifier			

(02) USING THE MODIFIERS :

In Bengali there are 13 Modifiers including Vowel-signs and others. In SUS script the modifiers have been designed with one horizontal line and a number of special signs, one representing each modifier.

In the vowel signs, a short line indicates Short (Hrasha) Vowel (like E ই, U উ etc.) and longer line, Long (Dirgha) Vowels (like , EE ঈ, UU ঊ etc.). The Vowel letters shown in Fig. 8.02 would appear exactly in this form when these will be used at the beginning of a word. Most of the times, however, the vowels are pronounced at the middle or end of the word. In such case, in Bengali not the vowels, but the vowel signs are used. These signs are joined with the consonant letters in 6 different places, viz. : (i) Before, (ii) After, (iii) Above, (iv) Below, (v) Both before and after and (vi) Both above and below the consonant letter.

In SUS script the vowel-sign would be used in the middle of the consonant letter. The middle of the SUS consonant letters have been kept free for this purpose. So there will be absolutely no problem in using the vowel and other signs there. In Bengali at times two consonant letters are pronounced at one time. Earlier such words were joined together by breaking certain parts of both. In view of tremendous problems in machine compose and hand writing, those are now combined together by using a sign known as Hasanta ৃ). This one also has been added in the list of modifier.

Even though it is possible to pronounce almost all the words by independent use of consonants, the same cannot serve the purpose at present served by three signs (Fala's), viz. (01) Ra-fala, (02) Ja-fala and (03) Hri-fala. In order to satisfy these modifying actions these three signs have been provided in the tray of Vowel signs. In fact the first two (i.e. Ra-fala and Ja-fala) are consonant signs and the last one (Hri-fala) is a vowel sign. Now it is possible to write and pronounce any or all of the Bengali words by using SUS script. The Vowels, Vowel-signs and Consonant signs of SUS scripts have been shown in **Fig. No. 8.02.**

In SUS, all the letters have been composed within a square. Even though the numbers (Digits) also have been composed within squares, those can be transformed into rectangles also. At present the scripts of some languages (like English, Bengali, Urdu, Arabic etc.) quite often show the following anomalies :

(i) The letters vary in width,

(ii) Some letters extend below the upper margin and some, below the lower margin.

(iii) Some of the vowel signs need to be attached above, below, before, after or both before and after the consonant letter.

These anomalies create severe problem in machine-compose and printing. The SUS script is completely free from these hazards because all SUS scripts have been designed within a square. Also even if any additional element needs to be added those can be done well within the boundary of the square.

Chapter IX

USING "SUS" IN ARABIC LANGUAGE

INTRODUCTION :

Even though Arabic language is a bit complex in comparison with English, it is possible to fulfil all the requirements of this language through SUS script. We shall present the solutions in the following stages : (01) Studying Arabic language, (02) Knowing the principal letters, (03) Knowing he Modifiers and (04) Using SUS scripts in writing Arabic language.

(01) STUDYING ARABIC LANGUAGE :

Like any other language Arabic is constituted of a number of principal letters (both consonants and Vowels) and a number of modifiers. Some of the specialities of this language are :

(i) The language is written from right to left,

(ii) The language is written by straight and curved strokes and dots.

(iii) There are systems for combining and using 2 or 3 principal letters.

(iv) Some of the principal letters have long pronunciation, which are done either by using modifiers or by other arrangement.

(v) The same word may be pronounced differently due to short or long sounding letters and in most cases those bear different meaning.

(02) KNOWING THE PRINCIPAL LETTERS :

There are 28 principal letters in Arabic. These have been presented along with their sounds (pronunciation) in English letters in **Fig. 9.01** below.

Fig. No. 9.01 ARABIC ALPHABET – PRINCIPAL LETTERS :

Sl. No	ARABIC LETTER	Pronunciation In English	Consonant sound	Sl. No	ARABIC LETTER	Pronunciation In English	Consonant sound
15	ض	(Daad)	Da	01	ا	(alif)	a
16	ط	(Toa)	Ta	02	ب	(baa)	Ba
17	ظ	(joa)	Ja	03	ت	(taa)	Ta
18	ع	(ayn)	Na	04	ث	(thaa)	Ta
19	غ	(ghayn)	Ga	05	ج	(Jiim)	Ja
20	ف	(faa)	Fa	06	ح	(Haa)	Ha
21	ق	(qaaf)	Ka	07	خ	(Khaa)	Kha
22	ك	(kaaf)	Ka	08	د	(daal)	Da
23	ل	(laam)	La	09	ذ	(jal)	Ja
24	م	(miim)	Ma	10	ر	(raw)	Ra
25	ن	(nuun)	Na	11	ز	(jha)	Jha
26	و	(waaw)	Wa	12	س	(siin)	Sa
27	ه	(haa)	Ha	13	ش	(shiin)	Sha
28	ي	(yaa)	Ya	14	ص	(Saad)	Sa

(03) KNOWING THE MODIFIERS :

The Arabic language has the following 11 modifiers, who modify the pronunciations of the principal letters. These modifiers along with their modifying actions have been shown in **Fig. No. 9.02.**

Fig. No. 9.02 MODIFIERS OF ARABIC LETTERS

NNo	MODIFIER	SIGN	MODIFYING ACTION	
01	Jabar		This is placed above the consonant and it adds u (as in but) or aa sound.	
02	Jer		This is placed below the consonant and it adds e (as in pet) sound.	
03	Pesh			This is placed above the consonant and it adds u (as in put) sound.
04	Double Jabar			This is placed above and it adds un (as in bun) sound.
05	Double Jer		This is placed below the consonant and it adds in (as in inn) sound.	
06	Double Pesh			This is placed above the consonant and it adds oon (as in moon) sound.

07	Sakin	------	There is no sign for Sakin. But three letters ‏أ‏ (alif), ‏و‏ (waaw) and ‏ي‏(yaa) are pronounced with a lingering sound when (a) Jabar is placed on the letter after ‏أ‏ (alif), (b) Pesh is placed on the letter before ‏و‏ (waaw), and (c) Jer is placed on the letter before ‏ي‏(yaa).
08	Jajam	∧	This is placed above the letter. When placed in any letter it is pronounced jointly with the previous letter.
09	Tasdid	W	This is placed above the letter and makes double sound.

(04) USING SUS SCRIPTS IN WRITING THE PRINCIPAL ARABIC LETTERS :

In using SUS script for writing the Arabic letters and modifiers we shall first divide the principal letters into groups of five, find out the group heads for each group and assign numerical identity for each letter. All these have been shown in **Fig. No. 9.03.**

Fig. No. 9.03 LOCATIONAL IDENTITY FOR PRINCIPAL ARABIC LETTERS :

.4	.3	.2	.1	.0	Group
‏ج‏ (Jiim)	‏ث‏ (thaa)	‏ت‏ (taa)	‏ب‏ (baa)	‏أ‏ (alif)	

					01
1.4	1.3	1.2	1.1	1.0	

					02
ر (raw)	ذ (jal)	د (daal)	خ (Khaa)	ح (Haa)	
2.4	2.3	2.2	2.1	2.0	

					03
ض (Daad)	ص (Saad)	ش (shiin)	س (siin)	ز (jha)	
3.4	3.3	3.2	3.1	3.0	

					04
ف (faa)	غ (ghayn)	ع (ayn)	ظ ((joa)	ط (Toa)	
4.4	4.3	4.2	4.1	4.0	

					05
ن (nuun)	م (miim)	ل (laam)	ك (kaaf)	ق (qaaf)	
5.4	5.3	5.2	5.1	5.0	

			06
ي (yaa)	ه (haa)	و (waaw)	
6.2	6.1	6.0	

In the above Table various Letters have got identity due to locations like, م (miim) is **5.3**, و (waaw) is **6.0** and so on. After learning these identities of the Arabic letters, the learner would have to replace those by SUS scripts. This has been shown in Fig. No. 8.02

In the above Table various Letters have got identity due to locations. So, 'miim' (م) has the identity **5.3**, 'waaw' (و) has got **6.0** and so on. After learning the identities of each of the Arabic letters, the learner would have to replace those by SUS scripts with corresponding number as shown in Fig. No. 8.02. The Arabic letters and their corresponding SUS script has been shown in **Fig. No. 9.04.**

Fig. No. 9.04 ARABIC LETTERS WRITTEN BY SUS :

.4	.3	.2	.1	.0	Group
ج (Jiim)	ث (thaa)	ت (taa)	ب (baa)	أ (alif)	
1.4	1.3	1.2	1.1	1.0	**01**

ر (raw)	ذ (Jal)	د (daal)	خ (Khaa)	ح (Haa)	
2.4	2.3	2.2	2.1	2.0	**02**

69

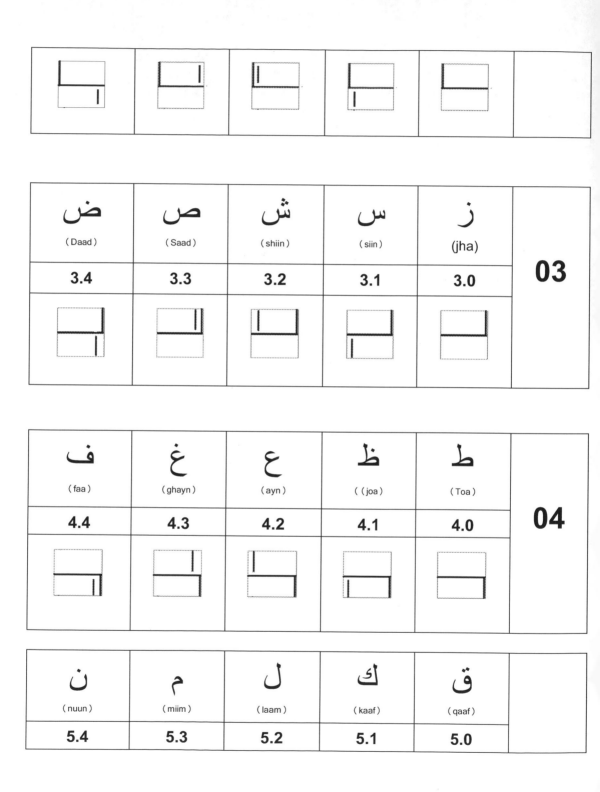

ض	ص	ش	س	ز	
(Daad)	(Saad)	(shiin)	(siin)	(jha)	**03**
3.4	3.3	3.2	3.1	3.0	

ف	غ	ع	ظ	ط	
(faa)	(ghayn)	(ayn)	((joa)	(Toa)	**04**
4.4	4.3	4.2	4.1	4.0	

ن	م	ل	ك	ق	
(nuun)	(miim)	(laam)	(kaaf)	(qaaf)	
5.4	5.3	5.2	5.1	5.0	

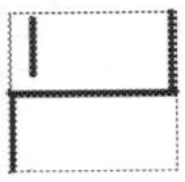

					05

ي	ه	و	
(yaa)	(haa)	(waaw)	**06**
6.2	**6.1**	**6.0**	

(05) USING SUS AS MODIFIRS :

The symbol, pronunciation and modifying action of the modifiers o Arabic language have been shown in **Fig. No. 9.05.**

Fig. No. 9.05 MODIFIERS :

Symbol	/		ᶨ	//		ᶨ	^	w
		\			\\	Nil		

Pronunciation in English	Jabar or Fatha	Jer or Kasra	Pesh or Jamma	Double Jabar	Double Jer	Double Pesh	Sakin	Jajam	Tasdid
Location of use	Above	Below	Above	Above	Below	Above	------	Above	Above
Modifying action	AA	E	OO	AAN	INN	OON	------	-----	Doubling

ASSIGNING SUS CRIPTS AS MODIFIERS :

The SUS scripts assigned as substitute for various modifiers of Arabic language have been shown in **Fig. 9.06.**

Fig. No. 9.06 SUS SCRIPTS TO BE USED AS MODIFIERS :

Symbol	/	＼	ꜟ	//	＼＼	ꜘ
Pronunciation in English	Jabar or Fatha	Jer or Kasra	Pesh or Jamma	Double Jabar	Double Jer	Double Pesh

Location of SUS modifier	Above	Below	Above	Above	Below	Above
Modifiers used in SUS	٠ٰ	٠	✝	۱	۱	✝

Symbol	Nil	∧	𝒲
Pronunciation in English	Sakin	Jajam	Tasdid
Location of SUS modifier	Above & below	Above	Above
Modifiers used in SUS			

Since the middle portion of the letter has been kept free, it is possible to use any of the 12 modifiers in this place. It is also possible to increase this number if need arises. Even though Sakin (the system in which three letters may have prolonged sound) does not have any sign in Arabic language, we have assigned one here. So, it will be possible to prolong the sound of not only these 3 letters, but of any Arabic letters by using it.

Chapter X

OTHER SCRIPTS

OTHER SCRIPTS :

The love men feel for their language or mother tongue is quite different from what they feel for the scripts they use for writing their languages. Many nations have abandoned their writing scripts because the users felt that those were difficult to write, prone to confusion, disadvantageous etc. The illiterate group of people cannot even feel any difference in their oral language due to such change. Some people who did not have 'fully developed alphabet' accepted the alphabet of another language. Thus the people belonging to 'Hausa tribe', living in northern Nigeria and speaking in a language known as 'Hausa language' accepted English alphabet for writing their language.

Taking this scope of such 'acceptability' of scripts, rather than oral language numerous endeavours were made in the past to design superior type of scripts. We shall mention hereunder two such scripts : (01) The Phags-pa script devised by a Tibetan Lama and (02) the Interbet Alphabet designed by Vitaly Vetash from Russia.

(01) Phags-pa script :

In 1260 Kublai Khan commissioned a Tibetan Lama to create a new national script. He devised the Phags-pa script in 1269. Notable features of this script, as alleged by the designer are :

(i) Syllabic alphabet : each consonant have an inherent vowel sound. Other vowels are indicated by symbols that appear below the consonants.

(ii) Writing direction : vertical from top to bottom and from left to right.

(iii) There were three different styles of writing in the Phags-pa alphabet: (a) the Standard script, which was used in Chinese and Mongolian printed texts and documents, (b) the Seal script, which was used mainly for official seals and also for some inscriptions on monuments and (c) the Tibetan script style, which was used mainly for books titles and temple inscriptions.

We present hereunder the first two types in **Fig. No. 10.01** and **Fig. No. 10.02.**

Fig. No. 10.01 Phags-pa STANDARD SCRIPT :

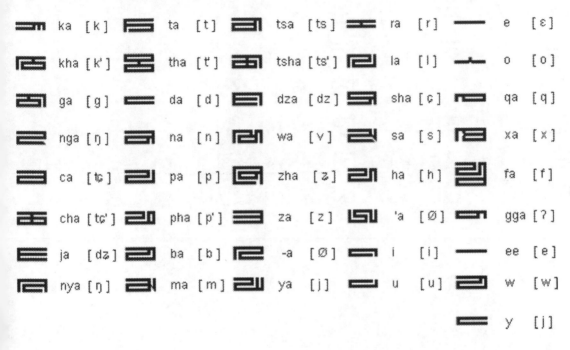

ka [k]   ta [t]   tsa [ts]   ra [r]   e [ɛ]

kha [k']   tha [t']   tsha [ts']   la [l]   o [o]

ga [g]   da [d]   dza [dz]   sha [ɕ]   qa [q]

nga [ŋ]   na [n]   wa [v]   sa [s]   xa [x]

ca [tɕ]   pa [p]   zha [ʐ]   ha [h]   fa [f]

cha [tɕ']   pha [p']   za [z]   'a [Ø]   gga [ʔ]

ja [dʐ]   ba [b]   -a [Ø]   i [i]   ee [e]

nya [ŋ]   ma [m]   ya [j]   u [u]   w [w]

y [j]

Fig. No. 10.02 Phags-pa SEAL SCRIPT :

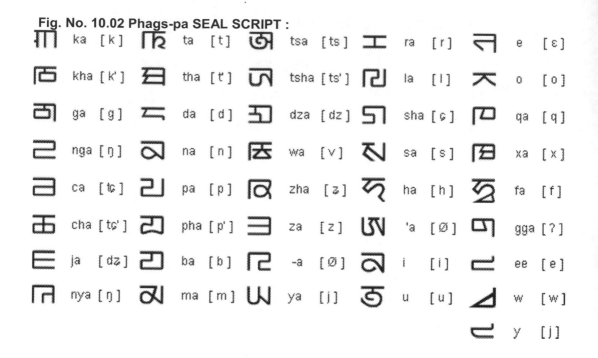

ka [k]	ta [t]	tsa [ts]	ra [r]	e [ɛ]
kha [kʼ]	tha [tʼ]	tsha [tsʼ]	la [l]	o [o]
ga [g]	da [d]	dza [dz]	sha [ɕ]	qa [q]
nga [ŋ]	na [n]	wa [v]	sa [s]	xa [x]
ca [tɕ]	pa [p]	zha [ʐ]	ha [h]	fa [f]
cha [tɕʼ]	pha [pʼ]	za [z]	ʼa [Ø]	gga [ʔ]
ja [dʑ]	ba [b]	-a [Ø]	i [i]	ee [e]
nya [ɳ]	ma [m]	ya [j]	u [u]	w [w]
				y [j]

N. B. : Courtesy and Source: http://babelstone.blogspot.com, Free Phags-pa fonts available   at   :
http://www.babelstone.co.uk/Fonts/   and
http://www.valdyas.org/conlang.html.

Further information about the Phags-pa Script may be collected from :
http://www.babelstone.co.uk/Phags-pa/

The pronunciations of some of the Phags-pa letters have similarities with those of Bengali letters. Most of the Bengali consonants are constituted of the bare minimum basic sound. Also a few Phags-pa letters looks like Bengali letters. While the Bengali consonants have been arranged in groups of 5, in Phags-pa those are in groups of 4. The cause of the above similarities between the two language might have been that both Bengali and Tibetan languages originated in some common languages.

CRITICISM : Even though the authors of Pags-pa script claimed that the scripts are easy, after looking at the scripts no one would believe it to be true. There is no logic in the gradual change of the letters, which has rendered these extremely difficult to remember. Even though it has been claimed that the direction of writing is "vertical from top to bottom and from left to right" it is not clear how these principles could be applied in writing the above letters.

(02) INTERBET :

Interbet is the abbreviation for 'International Phonematic Alphabet'. Vitaly Vetash, an artist and a linguist from Russia worked from 1977 to 1999 for creating this alphabet. As claimed, the names of the Interbet letters "are mostly based on the ancient Phoenician and Greek alphabets, as well as the letters of the other alphabets and on some practical names, traditional for linguists: with some changes, according to the principles of distinctivity from the other names, euphony and connection with a prototype".

The number of letters originally designed in this alphabet was 45. The contemporary version shows 50 capital and 50 small letters. The letters are based on the combination of Latin alphabet and some Cyrillic letters and some were invented by the author. The author proposed some linguistic signs also for modifying the sounds of the letters. In this system the same letters can be used to represent a number of phonemes.

According to the author, the number of letters is sufficient to write all of the world's most widely-spoken languages. The author also claimed that this alphabet was suitable for a practical, international and universal system for writing any language. It has been told the letters have taken into account the optic resonance between the shape of a letter and the characteristics of a phoneme.

Also claimed by the author "The main Interbet letters represent only one or two phonemes, while the additional letters (marked with 2 below) represent a greater range of phonemes. The usage of the marked letters depends on needs of each language. For example, it changes from plosive to fricative or aspirate consonant. The second sign for the vowel E (E2) always signifies a more open sound than the first E, despite the fact that in different languages these sounds will be different. In French the first E is the closed E <é> and the second E is open E <è> and in German they are e and ä respectively. T2 in English denotes /θ/, and in Hindi /th/". (Quoted from the original). The 45-letter alphabet of Interbet has been shown in **Fig. No. 10.03.**

Fig. No. 10.03 SUS ALPHABETS WITH LETTERS WITH SAME SOUNDS FROM OTHE
LANGUAGES :

Group		.0	.1	.2	.3	.4
01	SUS script and sound	KA	KHA	GA	GHA	RA
	ENGLISH script	K	--	G	---	R
	BENGALI script and sound	ক	খ	গ	ঘ	র
	ARABIC script and sound	ق	خ ,ك	غ	----	ر
02	SUS script and sound	CHA	CHHA	JA	JHA	LA
	ENGLISH script	C	--	J, Z	--	L
	BENGALI script and sound	চ	ছ	জ়	ঝ	ল
	ARABIC script and sound	---	---	ذ ,ج ,ظ	ز	ل
03	SUS script and sound	TA	THA	DA	DHA	NA
	ENGLISH script	T	--	D	--	N
	BENGALI script and sound	ট	ঠ	ড	ঢ	ন
	ARABIC script and sound	ت		د		ن

04	SUS script and sound	PA	FA	BA	BHA	MA
	ENGLISH script	P	F	B	V	M
	BENGALI script and sound	প	ফ	ব	ভ	ম
	ARABIC script and sound	---	ف	ب	---	م

05	SUS script and sound	(ta*) Pronounced like ট of Bengali	(tha*) Pronounced like থ of Bengali	(da*) Pronounced like দ of Bengali	(dha*) Pronounced like ধ of Bengal	(rha*)
	ENGLISH script	--	--	--	--	--
	BENGALI script and sound	ত	থ	দ	ধ	ড়
	ARABIC script and sound	ط	ث	ض	-----	-----

06	SUS script and sound	SA	SHA	HRI	ANG	HRA
	ENGLISH script	S	--	--	--	--
	BENGALI script and sound	স	শ	ষ	্ং	ঢ়
	ARABIC script and sound	ص ,س	ش	-----	-----	-----

07	SUS script and sound	EE	U or OO	A	O	MN
	ENGLISH script	E	U	A	O	--
	BENGALI script and sound	ই	উ	এ	ও	==
	ARABIC script and sound	---	---	---	و	---

08	SUS script and sound	AA	E	A	HA	OY
	ENGLISH script	U	E	A	H	Y
	BENGALI script and sound	আ	ই	য্যা	হ	ওয়
	ARABIC script and sound	أ	---	---	ح, ہ	ع, ي

Source : http://www.astrolingua.spb.ru/ENGLISH/inter_eng.htm and semiravet@yandex.ru

CRITICISM : From a peer look at the above letters most of the claims about its superiority do not seem to be true. A number of 100 letters seems too many for any language to be easy and efficient. It is not clear how such an alphabet can be used in writing any language of the world.

Chapter IX

CONCLUSION

INTRODUCTION :

Language had to be created immediately after the appearance of men in this world. It is one of the oldest items men started using and shall be doing the same for all time to come. In order to suit new situations the users of some languages have modified their oral and written languages from time to time. However, no dignified nation or user-group ever thinks of completely abandoning their language for the purpose of accepting a new one, whatever disadvantageous their own language might have been. As a member of this world we should show proper respect to others' languages. Such a reality should discourage all who think of, or endeavour to devise means of eliminating others mother tongue. In such a situation the proposed SUS can present before all languages the following two options :

Option 01 : The user of the language who might discover their alphabet difficult to pronounce and/or disadvantageous to write may take up the SUS alphabets. This would not bring about any major change in their oral language. It has been mentioned that languages may be of several types like those (i) using only letters, (ii) using letters and signs, (iii) using two types of letters, viz. Capital and small etc. SUS alphabets can be used to speak and write all these languages, without, however, using separate capital letters or any type of signs. And all these can be done by using maximum 40 letters.

Option 02 : The user of any language who might feel their alphabet difficult to remember, tiresome and slow to write, not free from the teachers criticism of "bad handwriting", prone to creating confusion etc. may accept SUS scripts only for writing their languages. The SUS scripts has provisions for accommodating all types of languages including those (i) having two types of letters, Capital and small), (ii) having only one type of letters, (iii) with vowels and consonants with different types of use, (iv) having vowel signs to be used with the consonant and vowel letters, (vi) those writing from left to right or vice versa. If accepted SUS would bring no, we repeat, absolutely no change in the oral language including its grammar and other uses.

SCRIPTS AND HANDWRITING

The first and foremost need of the script is in handwriting. In the contemporary world the most widely used scripts fall under the following groups :

(01) Writing by long hand with or without dots and strokes,

(02) Writing by straight stroke with or without dots and strokes,

(03) Writing by curved stroke and shapes with or without dots and strokes and

(04) Combinations thereof.

In general long-line writings are speedier than the stroke-types. However, both have advantages and disadvantages as shown below.

LONG WRITINGS : (i) Generally speedier, but the more is the speed the more is the possibilibity of confusion leading to wrong message.

(ii) The more is the number of extra dots and strokes the slower will be the speed.

(iii) The more is the number of signs the less will be the speed.

STROKE WRITINGS : (i) Generally slower, the less is the number of stroke the more is the speed.

(ii) The more is the number of stroke the more is the possibility of confusion.

(iii) The more is the number of extra dot and stroke the slower is the speed.

In **Fig. No. 11.01** below we show important features of the scripts of some languages in connection with preferences in writing by hand. These would easily reveal their relative advantages and disadvantages.

Fig. No. 11.01 IMPORTANT FEATURES OF THE SCRIPTS OF SOME LANGUAGES IN CONNECTION WITH PREFERENCES IN WRITING

LANGUAGE	LETTERS HAVING SIMILAR SOUNDS	USE OF LETTERS IN WORDS	TYPE OF WRITING, LINE OR STROKE	USE OF DOTS / EXTRA-STROKES ETC.
English	*Yes, some letters	**Independent letters, almost all can be joined in long hand	***Long line with circular, elliptical, triangular, straight and curved lines	****2 dots, 1 cut
Bengali	*Yes, some letters	**Independent letters, many can be joined in long hand	***Long line with circular, elliptical, triangular, straight and curved lines	****4 dots, many signs
Arabic	*Yes, some letters	**Independent letters, some may be joined in long hand	***Long line with circular, elliptical, triangular, straight and curved lines	****Many dots and signs
SUS	All letters have single sound	Independent letters. Little possibility of joining.	Only 2 to 4 nos. strokes per letter.	None. But when SUS scripts are used to write languages with signs, it gets slower.

* This creates confusion in hearing and then writing.

** Joining increases speed and at the same time possibility of confusion and illegibility.

*** These shapes change due to human effort and lead to "bad/good handwriting" situation.

**** The more the number of dots/signs, the slower will be the speed.

SCRIPTS AND TYPE SETTING (KEYBOARDS)

In the contemporary world, printing or typing letters is equally or may be more important than writing those by hand. Naturally the quality of any alphabet to type easily and swiftly is to be considered with extreme importance. In this regard the languages with less number of letters, those using only letters and those requiring same-sized space and those not extending the margins may be in preferable positions. The languages using vowel signs have particular problem in typing. In **Fig. No. 11.02** we show the notable features of the scripts of some languages. These would reveal the relative advantages and disadvantages of these languages in typing/printing.

Fig. No. 11.02 NOTABLE FEATURES OF THE SCRIPTS OF SOME LANGUAGES.

LANGUAGE	NO. OF LETTERS*	TYPE OF LETTERS**	TYPE OF SPACE REQUIRED***	WHETHER EXTENDS BEYOND MARGINS****
English	26 + 26	Capital and small letters	Letters vary in height and breadth	Extends
Bengali	35 + 12 +12(sign)+	Vowels, consonants, vowel signs, other signs etc.	Letters vary in height and breadth	Extends

Arabic	28 + 9(signs)	Letters and vowel signs	Letters vary in height and breadth	Extends
SUS*	40	Only letters	All equal size	Does not extend

* The more the number of letters the more will be the need of keys in keyboards and types.

** The more the types of letters and signs the more difficult is typing. Typing of vowel sign is problematic and reduces typing speed.

*** Varying space create problem.

**** Extension beyond margin creates problem.

KEY BOARDS FOR VARIOUS LANGUAGES :

In the modern age at times we need use small key boards. In this case the less is the number of key the easier it will be to type the language. It has been mentioned that SUS uses only a few strokes in typing the letters. So, in typing SUS scripts, the keys will be used for typing the various strokes only. Naturally the number of keys will be quite less even if the number of letters is many. We present hereunder an account of the minimum number of keys required to type some languages using SUS script.

ENGLISH LANGUAGE : This language uses 56 letters belonging to Capital and Small cases and no modifiers.

(01) In SUS the number of keys required for typing 26 letters will be :

   (i) 1 key for typing the central horizontal line.

   (ii) 4 keys or 1 navigation key for typing the small and free vertical lines at four locations. When these 4 keys or the navigation will be pressed, first they would give the small vertical line, and then the free vertical line.

85

Or alternate for (1) and (ii) : 6 keys for group heads and 1 navigation key.

(iii) 1 key for typing the sign for capital letters.

So, the total number of keys required will be 3 to 7.

(02) For typing 10 DIGITS we would need the following keys :

(i) 1 key for typing the long vertical horizontal line.

(ii) 2 keys or 1 navigation key for typing the small horizontal lines at two extremities.

(iii) 2 keys or the above navigation key for typing the internal small horizontal lines.

So, the total number of keys required will be 4 to 5.

If independent keys are used for the above two purposes, the total number of required keys will be : 7 to 12.

BENGALI LANGUAGE : Bengali language use (i) (35 + 10 =) 45 principal letters and (ii) 13 modifiers. The no. of keys required for typing these will be :

(01) In SUS script the number of keys required for typing 45 principal letters will be :

(i) 1 key for typing the central horizontal line.

(ii) 1 key for typing the long vertical lines on left.

(iii) 4 keys or 1 Navigation key for typing the small vertical or free vertical lines at four locations. When these 4 keys or the navigation will be pressed, first they would give the small vertical line, and then the free vertical line.

Or alternate for (1), (ii) and (iii) : 9 keys for group heads and 1 navigation key. So, the total number of keys required will be 3 to 9.

(02) The number of keys required for typing 13 modifiers will be : 13 single keys or 7 double option keys. So, the total number of keys for the above 2 purposes will be 10 to 22.

ARABIC LANGUAGE : In Arabic language there are : (i) 28 principal letters and (ii) 9 modifiers.

(01) The number of keys required for typing 28 principal letters will be :

> (i) 1 key for typing the central horizontal line.
>
> (ii) 4 keys or 1 Navigation key for typing the small vertical or free vertical lines at four locations. When these 4 keys or the navigation will be pressed, first they would give the small vertical line, and then the free vertical line.

Or alternate for (1) and (ii) : 6 keys for group heads and 1 navigation key.

So, the total number of keys required will be 2 to 5.

(02) The number of keys required for typing 9 modifiers will be : 9 single keys or 5 double option keys.

So, the total number of keys required for the above purposes will be 7 to 14.

KEY BOARDS FOR VARIOUS PURPOSES :

Key boards are required for various purposes. For example, small-size key board with minimum number of Keys is required for the Mobile phones. Again, key board with minimum number of keys arranged in a larger space is advantageous for the blinds. For typing in typewriters and computers, there is no dearth of space and no constraint on the number of keys. Now we shall see how SUS can be of use in the above gadgets.

(01) MOBILE PHONE : For ease of making telephone call the mobile phones must have 10 keys. Also those need the 4-way Navigation key for normal operation. The minimum number of keys for writing various languages in SUS script are the following :

SL. NO.	LANGUAGE	OPERATION	TYPE AND NUMBER OF KEYS		
			Navigation Type	Normal type	Total (Normal)
01	SUS	Typing 40 letters	1 key	3 normal	03
02	English	Typing 52 letters	1	4 normal (1 for the capital words)	04
03	Bengali	Typing 45 principal letters and 13 moderators	1	4 normal + 3 keys for 13 modifiers @ 3 per key.	07
04	Arabic	Typing 28 principal letters and 9 moderators	1	3 normal + 5 keys for 9 modifiers @ 2 per key	08

It is seen that the above 4 languages can be written by using only 3 to 8 keys, which are well below 10.

As for script, in the normal operation the mobile needs to have characters for all the letters of all the languages it would write or transmit. In the above case the job may be finished by storing maximum 45 characters for letters and 13 for modifiers. That means all languages of the world can be written with total 58 characters.

(02) FOR THE BLIND : In the key board to be used by the blinds, small size is not essential. The less the number of keys the easier it is for the blinds. It has been shown that it is possible to write or type various languages with less number of keys. If we discard the use of navigation key (to be substituted by 4 normal keys) and 2/3 way keys, then they can write SUS language by using 7 keys, English language by 8 keys, Bengali language by 21 keys and Arabic language by 16 keys and so on.

(03) COMPUTER KEY BOARD : In the conventional key board for computer 26 double option keys have been kept for typing 52 English letters. If only one key is kept reserved for typing one character, then the number of keys for writing the following 4 languages in SUS script will be :

(i) SUS 40 nos., (ii) English 27 nos., (iii) Bengali 48 nos. and (iv) Arabic 19 nos.

If the current system of double option keys are retained, then the number keys required will be :

(i) SUS 20 nos., (ii) English 14 nos., (iii) Bengali 24 nos. and (iv) Arabic 10 nos.

OBJECTIVE OF DESIGNING SUS :

SUS was designed on the basis of the following considerations and objectives :

(01) The prime responsibility of a language is to transfer ideas and its success depends upon how swiftly and faultlessly its scripts can convey the same to others.

(02) In the contemporary age machine writing (i.e. typing or printing) of message is equally important like writing.

(03) Confusion in transferring message is a serious issue and may result in disaster unless eliminated. In case o handwriting, eliminating it is much more important than the speed of writing.

(04) For the kids the objective of learning language is to lean various subjects of knowledge. When the questions of good / bad handwriting, clumsy, illegible etc. are attached to the writings of the learners they feel demoralized. Any system capable of

eliminating this hazard may be considered as a welcome proposition.

(05) Experiences reveal that the 'scripts written by stroke' are better than those by long lines, because the first one is free from many criticisms and problems caused due to natural human error.

(06) Many scripts have been criticised for occupying varying width and height of letters and for using space beyond the margins. SUS letters occupies square space and does not exceed the border lines.

(07) Experiences reveal that the less is the number of strokes or signs, the easier it is to learn, write and read. Most of the SUS letters have been written with 2 to 4 strokes.

Even though initially the authors did not have any intention to design a script that could write all languages of this world, later it was found that the script designed was capable of writing most, if not all the languages of the world.

A peer look at the scripts might convince any person that SUS is capable of lessening considerable portion of the time and exertion of the learners. Also it would be able to save huge stationary now spent all over the world for the purpose of learning the alphabets.

Once a person becomes proficient in SUS, it will be extremely easy for him to read other languages written by the same script.

INTERNATIONAL LANGUAGE VERSUS UNIFIED SCRIPT :

After men came to realize the titanic barrier the language created between various countries and regions, there were many endeavours to devise "universal or international language", "unified script" etc. The brightest aspect of such an international language is, it is capable of making all people of the world conversant with one another. At the same time, its darkest aspect is, in doing so it would kill all the languages men created in various regions and countries. It is inhuman even to think of the death of a language, whatever small might be the number of its users. Language is the invaluable gift given to its users by their ancestors. Men in general love their mother language. Some of them love it so dearly that they do not hesitate to sacrifice lives for its cause.

In such a situation, whereas international language brings death to numerous languages, the unified script helps all of them not only to survive, but also to live with increased efficiency. This quality is achieved due to the simplicity, logic and numerical relation applied in the design of the scripts. Written scripts act simply as a medium of documentation and non-personal communication. The illiterate people are completely ignorant of this system and still they enjoy all the conveniences and blessings of language. If a single script can replace all other scripts, then this also would help in bonding the relation between the strangers. Also it may help the manufacturers of various gadgets (viz. mobile phone, computer etc.) in manufacturing their products more easily and at less expense.

However, in order to attain acceptance and popularity the unified script must not bring any change in the oral language. The first and foremost condition of keeping the oral language exactly the same is to retain the original alphabet of the language. SUS ensures that by replacing the script and not the sound.

Universal language, Unified language, International language or whatever name is given to any new alphabet, it turns international and universal only after considerable number of users from various languages accepts it. And such users would use it only after they would find it easy and efficient. Thus, the best way to test the capability of any new script is to introduce and make it available to the users.

SUS is now in the field and it is fully prepared to face the challenge and appear in the examination. The users would compare its relative advantage and disadvantage before taking decision.

Whatever logic we might present, some users may always feel reluctant to accept a new thing like SUS. They may do so on the plea that it might throw away the long nurtured scripts, for which they have grown emotional attachment. Even though it may be a good reason for rejection of SUS, saving the learner's pains and time and huge quantity of scarce resources of this world might be a better reason in favour of its acceptance.

THE END

Authors

Prof. Bijon B. Sarma is an architect and a writer. At present he is the professo
the Department of Architecture, University of Khulna, Bangladesh.
His writings include a big number of Text Books for the students of Architec
Books on designs and plans of low housing, Urban Planning, low cost air co
system housing and many others, in the field of fictions quite a number of b
including two published by Trafford are "Journey to the East" and " The Drum-
Migration.
Dr. Mira R. Sarma-Parai is a Pathologist by profession in Alberta, Canada, ma
the books she co - authored with her brother Bijon.

LANGUAGE	SCRIPT	SCRIPT	SCRIPT	SCRIPT	SCRIPT		SCRIP
ENGLISH	Ka	Kha	Ga	Gha	Ta		Th
BENGALI	ক	থ	গ	ঘ	ট		ঠ
ARABIC	ق	خ	غ	ك	ط,ت		-----